POSITIVE
PSYCHOLOGY
FOR IMPROVING
MENTAL HEALTH
&
WELL-BEING

Dr. GEETIKA PATNAIK

INDIA • SINGAPORE • MALAYSIA

Notion Press

No. 8, 3rd Cross Street,
CIT Colony, Mylapore,
Chennai, Tamil Nadu – 600 004

First Published by Notion Press 2021
Copyright © Dr. Geetika Patnaik 2021
All Rights Reserved.

ISBN 978-1-63806-512-8

Dedication

I dedicate this book to my mother, Renuka. My mother's love has always been a sustaining force in my life. I am reminiscing and visualizing her positivity in her every action while writing this book. I have seen her walking straight with head held high no matter how zigzag and uncertain was her life's journey. She is my role model who was the epitome of grace and positivity. I have learnt from her that

Positivity is a choice; not an entitlement.

I am optimistic and hopeful that this book will be helpful to my readers in leading a stress-free, engaged, and peaceful life.

Contents

Preface *9*

1. History of Positive Psychology **11**

The First Wave: The Disease Model 12
The Second Wave: Behaviourism 12
The Third Wave: Existential and Humanistic Psychology 13
The Fourth Wave: Positive Psychology 15

2. Pioneers of Positive Psychology **23**

Abraham Maslow's Contribution to Positive Psychology 23
How to Improve Self-Efficacy 33

3. Contribution of Martin Seligman to Positive Psychology ... **39**

Four Levels of Analysis for Positive Psychology 41
Seligman's PERMA Model 41
Flourishing: Product of Pursuit and Engagement 43
Seligman's Manual on Character Strengths and Virtues 44

4. Positive Emotions **53**

Broaden – and – Build theory of Fredrickson 54
Positive Emotions Facilitate Psychological Well-Being 58

5. Positive Traits and Positive Subjective Experiences.............65

Major Positive Traits...67

Characteristics of the Creative Personality 69

6. Flow and Happiness...79

Meaning and Nature of Happiness...86

Theories of Happiness...91

The Set-Point Theory of Happiness 91

Life Satisfaction and Affective State Theories 93

7. Altruism, Hope and Optimism 97

Altruism and Prosocial Behaviour 98

Nepotistic Altruism...99

Reciprocal Altruism 99

Cognitive Reasons and Altruism 99

Optimism and Health..106

Positive Illusions and Mood 108

Learned Optimism...110

Increasing Optimism..110

8. Positive Thinking and Resilience 115

Explanatory Style and Positive Thinking 116

Enhancing Resilience in Childhood 123

Enhancing Resilience in Adulthood 124

9. Emotional Intelligence..127

Importance of Emotional Intelligence 132

10. Stress and Its Management **137**

Signs and Symptoms of Stress 138

Physical Symptoms of Stress 139

Emotional Symptoms of Stress 139

Cognitive Symptoms of Stress 140

Behavioural Symptoms of Stress 140

External Stressors 141

Internal Stressors 141

Effects of Chronic Stress 142

Stress and Disease 143

Coping with Stress 148

Factors Influencing Coping Strategies 150

Stress Management Strategies 153

11. Mental Health and Psychological Well-Being **159**

Issues and Challenges of Mental Health 160

Approaches to Mental Health Issues 162

Biopsychosocial Approach 162

Prevention and Interventions 163

Reducing Health-Compromising Behaviours 163

Increasing Health-Enhancing Behaviour 164

Tips for Good Mental Health 164

Factors Affecting Well-Being 175

12. Ways to Positive Psychology **179**

Mindfulness 187

Sustaining Activities and Experiences 189

The Imagined Self-Technique 191

Strength-Building Measures 192

Meaning-Oriented PPI 192

13. Helping Positivity **195**

Physical Benefits of Yoga 201

Social Dimension of Yoga.. 202

Emotional Dimension of Yoga 204

Spiritual Dimension of Yoga 206

Questions *209*

References *225*

Preface

Positive Psychology is psychology with positive orientation dealing with authentic happiness and good life. The key constructs related to positive psychology include character strengths, positive emotions, happiness and flow, hope and optimism, resilience, and well-being. The person who is mentally healthy can cope with all kinds of challenges in life. Well-being implies good mental health, high level of life-satisfaction, and the ability to manage stress. Precursors to positive psychology like altruism, optimism, and emotional intelligence imbibe positivity. The importance of Positive Psychology Interventions (PPIs) and the benefits of *Yoga* in promoting strength, endurance, and overall well-being have been analysed in detail. The book conveys the positive message:

Positivity should be inculcated consciously to achieve psychological growth which is basic to overall well-being.

History of Positive Psychology

The formal title **Positive Psychology** referring to a specific discipline within the field of Psychology has only existed since the year 2000. However, the various concepts that constitute the basis of positive psychology have been present in philosophical discourse for thousands of years. In an address to the American Psychological Association 1908 William James raised the issue that why some people live fully engaged lives compared to other people. The term **Positive Psychology** dates back to 1954, when Maslow's first edition of, **"Motivation and Personality"** was published with a final chapter titled, **"Toward a positive Psychology"**. There have been signs that psychologists since 1950s have been increasingly interested on the promotion of mental health rather than treating mental illnesses. After the Second World War, the focus of psychology was on treating abnormal behaviours and the resulting mental illnesses. Humanist psychologists like Abraham Maslow, Carl Rogers, and Eric Fromm were not satisfied with this approach and they were more concerned to study the positive aspects of human nature. Psychology had already been tagged with a negative panorama for its focus on the dark chambers of human mind and negligence of its sunlit highlands. Positive psychology, as the name suggests, is psychology with a positive orientation. We have to go into detail the three waves of psychology that came prior to positive psychology in order to know the roots of positive psychology.

The First Wave: The Disease Model

During the second half of the 19th Century and the early part of the 20th Century psychology was concerned with curing mental disorders. The attempt of psychologists to cure these ailments was praise-worthy and the work of early psychologists such as Freud, Adler, and Jung was indeed very effective in treating mental patients. Gradually, this **disease- oriented model** of psychology focused the dark cavities of the human mind and neglected the deeper well- springs of human energy and potential. It was observed by Maslow (1954) that the science of psychology has been far more successful on the negative than on the positive side. It has disclosed to us much about man's shortcomings, illnesses, and abnormalities; but little about his potentialities, virtues, achievable aspirations or his full psychological height. It is as if psychology has intentionally confined itself to only half its rightful dominion, and that; the darker and the meaner half.

The Second Wave: Behaviourism

J.B. Watson, Ivan Pavlov and B.F. Skinner were pioneers of behavioural approach in psychology. **Behaviourism**, according to Watson, was the science of observable behaviour. Watson argued that a child's environment is the factor that shapes behaviours over his / her genetic makeup or natural temperament. Watson's behaviourist theory did not focus on the internal emotional and psychological conditions of people, but rather on their external and outward behaviours. Watson is also known for the little Albert experiment, in which he demonstrated that a child could be conditioned to fear a previously neutral stimulus. The main goal of behaviourism is to predict and control behaviour. It is an approach introduced by Watson that emphasizes only upon measuring observable behaviour as a means of studying psychology.

Pavlov's contribution to psychology had a profound and lasting influence on the science of mind and behaviour. His discovery of classical conditioning helped establish the school of thought known as behaviourism. Behaviourism is a theory of learning which states all behaviours are learned through interaction with the environment through a process called conditioning. The behaviourists were of opinion that a person's behaviour was determined only by his life long history of rewards and punishments. In other words, actions that had been rewarded were likely to be repeated and actions that had been punished were likely to be suppressed.

According to Skinner, behaviourism is primarily concerned with observable behaviour, as opposed to internal events like thinking and emotion. Skinner viewed that given the right structure of rewards and punishments, human behaviour could be totally modified and moulded in an almost mechanical way. In other words, human being is entirely shaped by his external environment i.e. by rewards and punishments rather than by his internal thoughts. This idea of operant conditioning for shaping and eliciting desired behaviour through a well-designed reward system has a lot of merits. All human actions, Skinner believed was the direct result of conditioning. Behaviourists usually ignore the genetic makeup and internal factors like motivation and emotion in their approach to study behaviour. Skinner has explained the child's development as a creative process facilitated by parental acceptance and love. For example, saying 'Thank you' does not come naturally to children. They must learn to emit this response. Parents on the first occasion of emission of 'thank you' by their child usually bestow abundant praise and affection on the child. These environmental events constitute reinforcing conditions and serve to strengthen the 'thank you' response. Skinner in his book "Freedom and Dignity" views that human behaviour is not spontaneous but determined or controlled by education, advertisement, propaganda, and by the reinforcement contingencies operating in our environment.

The Third Wave: Existential and Humanistic Psychology

This wave is known for its two major streams of thought i.e. Existentialist psychology and Humanistic Psychology. Every human being is responsible for working out his/ her identity and life's meaning through interaction between self and his/ her surroundings. For this reason life's meaning is something truly unique to each person i.e. separate and independent. Individuals have to work out on the meaning of life for themselves, through their own unique experiences and surroundings. It becomes an issue when people fail to find their identity and their life's meaning. In such cases, overwhelming anxiety is inevitable and this anxiety is recognized in psychotherapy as, **existential anxiety** and has been of major therapeutic concern. The humanistic movement is about adding a holistic dimension to psychology. Humanistic psychologists viewed that our behaviour is determined by our perception of the world around us and its meanings. It makes us realize that we are not simply the product of our environment or biochemistry, and that we are intrinsically influenced and motivated to fulfil our human potential. **Humanistic psychology** emphasizes the inherent human drive towards self-actualization i.e. the process of realizing and expressing one's own capabilities and creativity. This approach became popular in the mid 20th Century in response to the restrictions of the disease model in fulfilling the human desire for actualization and a life of meaning. The five principles of humanistic psychology are:

- Human beings, as human, surpass the sum of their parts. They cannot be reduced to components.
- Human beings have their existence in a uniquely human context as well as in a cosmic ecology.
- Human beings are aware and are aware of 'being aware' i.e. they are conscious. Human consciousness always includes an awareness of oneself in the context of other people.
- Human beings have the ability to make choices and, therefore, have responsibility.
- Human beings are goal-directed. They aim at goals, are aware that they cause future events and seek meaning, value, and creativity.

One can notice the significant foundation that the humanistic approach has provided for positive psychology. Several humanistic psychologists, most notably Maslow, Rogers, and Fromm (1973) developed theories and practices pertaining to human happiness and flourishing. Of late, positive psychologists have found empirical support for the humanistic theories of flourishing. In addition, positive psychology has moved ahead in a variety of new directions.

The Fourth Wave: Positive Psychology

It is already mentioned that positive psychology is psychology with a positive orientation dealing with authentic happiness and a good life. While the previous waves of psychology focused on human flaws, overcoming deficiencies, avoiding pain, and escape from unhappiness; positive psychology focuses on well-being, contentment, excitement, cheerfulness, the pursuit of happiness and meaning in life. The humanistic movement looked at what drives us to grow and achieve fulfilment. It is to be noted that while the humanistic approach used more qualitative methods; positive psychology is developing a more scientific knowledge of understanding human beings. In the year 1998, Martin Seligman was elected President of the American Psychological Association and positive psychology was the theme of his term as President. However, Seligman did not start the field alone and was not considered as the first positive psychologist. Besides Seligman, there have been other significant influencers who have contributed to this new era of psychology. Many consider William James to be the America's first positive psychologist because of his deep interest in the subjectivity of a person and he believed that "objectivity is based on intense subjectivity". James opined that in order to study a person's optimal functioning; one has to analyse how he/ she personally experiences the situation which is known as the subjective experience of the individual. James was interested in what was objective and observable which is termed as **radical empiricism**. The first positive psychology conference took place in 1999 and the first World Congress on positive psychology was held at the University of Pennsylvania in 2002. Even though positive psychology offers a new approach to the study of positive emotions and behaviour; the ideas, theories, research, and motivation to study the positive side of human behaviour is as old as humanity. Positive psychology revitalizes the positive aspects of human nature i.e. Positive subjective experiences, positive individual traits, and civic virtues (Seligman, Csikszentmihalyi, 2000). The human being should be conceptualized and understood as a 'being' with inherent potentials for developing positive character traits or virtues. This idea is the core of the actualizing tendency as described by Maslow (1968). For positive psychology, the concept of good character thus becomes the central concept.

Aristotelian tradition is the core root of positive Psychology. It concentrates on positive experiences and positive character or virtues. Aristotle's approach focuses on the positive human being who is not comfortable with the widely disseminated medical model with its purely negative frame of reference emphasizing failure, fault, illness, and classification of mental disorders. The individual is, hence, a being, who introduces positive goals and values and strives to realize and reach them. According to Aristotle, the individual is characterized by experiencing joy when exercising his or her inherent or acquired abilities and striving towards realizing them in ways that are experienced as better, more complex or more perfect. Aristotelian principle says that, "other things being equal, human beings enjoy the exercise of their realized capacities (their innate or trained abilities), and this enjoyment increases the more the capacity is realized, or the greater the complexity". Thus, it is the process of exercising that is central in the Aristotelian frame of reference. In line with this view, positive psychology supports that human beings enjoy the exercise of their capabilities. Positive psychology says that people get enjoyment or good feelings when they do accomplish something that stretches them beyond what they are i.e. excellence in sports, drama, academics or any other activities. The idea is that it is the enjoyment attached to the activity that leads to personal growth and long term happiness. Positive psychology clearly confirms the Aristotelian view that goodness and morality do not come from outside the person. Hence, these good qualities are not the product of cultural sources or of moral rules of society but originate from the potentials of the human being. In addition, positive psychology claims that strengths and virtues are to be nurtured by ourselves. Positive psychology also clings to a fundamental assumption that our living systems are self-organizing and oriented towards an elaborate and complex functioning. This process has been defined as cultivation. It not only promotes the growth of flow activities but the individual behaviour as a whole. Moreover, in both the Aristotelian and the positive psychology approaches, the concept of optimal functioning is associated with the concept of the good life, well-being or happiness. Aristotle model of the good life, **eudaimonia** is the state of being well and doing well in being well. Thus, for Aristotle, what constitutes the good for man is a complete human life lived at its best, and the exercise of the virtues is a necessary and central part of such a life. In positive psychology, however, there are two different approaches to the good life: **hedonic approaches** and **eudaimonic approaches.** The hedonic approach focuses on happiness in terms of pleasure attainment and pain avoidance. The eudemonic approach is concerned with the whole person and his or her optimal functioning and development in all areas of life. Some view positive psychology as a meeting of Eastern thought, such as Buddhism, and Western psychodynamic approaches. Positive psychology studies people's happiness rather than diagnosing mental illnesses and treating what makes them miserable. Nevertheless, the issue of suffering cannot be ignored. Positive psychologists just take a different approach to it.

Positive Psychology is the study of the good life or the positive aspects of the human experience that makes life worth living. Good life is defined as **optimal functioning and experience.** It is striving for perfection that represents the realization of one's true potential. Good life is well-being which arises when the individual is functioning optimally. The good life is thus characterized by development from simple to more complex or optimal functioning (Ryan & Deci, 2001). As an art, it focuses on both individual and societal well-being. Moreover, positive psychology is a reaction against psychoanalysis and behaviourism, which have focused on mental illnesses and highlighted maladaptive behaviour and negative thinking. It is greatly influenced by humanistic movement which emphasizes on happiness, well-being, and positivity. Seligman and Csikszentmihalyi (2000) define positive psychology as, "the scientific study of positive human functioning and flourishing on multiple levels that include the biological, personal, relational, institutional, cultural, and global dimensions of life". The field of positive psychology at the subjective level is about valued subjective experiences i.e. well-being, contentment and satisfaction (in the past); hope and optimism (for the future) and flow and happiness (in the present). At the individual level, it is about positive individual trait: the capacity for love and vocation, courage, interpersonal skills, aesthetic sensibility, perseverance, forgiveness, originality, future mindedness, spirituality, high talent, and wisdom. At the group level, it is about the civic virtues and the institutions that move individuals towards better citizenship, responsibility, nurturance, altruism, civility, moderation, tolerance, and work ethic (Seligman &Csikszentmihalyi, 2000). Hence, positive psychology is nothing more than the scientific study of ordinary human strengths and virtues. It revisits the 'average person' with an interest in finding out what works, what is right, and what is improving (Sheldon & King, 2001). Gable and Haidt (2005) stated that positive psychology is the study of the conditions and processes that contribute to the flourishing or optimal functioning of people, groups, and institutions. It is about scientifically informed perspectives on what makes life worth living. It focuses on aspects of human condition that led to happiness, fulfilment, and flourishing (Buck, et al. 2008). Some experts describe it as "nothing more than the scientific study of ordinary human strengths and virtues" (Seligman, 2003). Seligman observed that before World War-II. Psychology had three distinct goals. The first one was to cure mental illness. The second was to make everyone's life happier and more productive and fulfilling. The third was to identify and nurture high talent and genius. He informed that after the war, the last two of the missions were forgotten. Positive psychology aims at bringing attention back to the pursuit of happiness and the nurturing of genius and talent. Seligman believed that the time has finally arrived for a science that seeks to understand positive emotion, build strength and virtue, and provide guide posts for finding what Aristotle called the **good life**. The aim of positive psychology is to bring about a change in the focus of psychology from preoccupation only with repairing the worst things in life to building positive qualities. Hence, a positive psychological perspective for the discipline of psychology is that the focus of scientific research and interest should be on understanding the entire breadth of human experience; from loss, suffering, illness, and distress through connection, fulfilment, health and well-being. As such, positive psychology shifts the implicit value basis of psychological inquiry from only a deficit focus to an asset-focus and exposes what is often new and fertile ground for investigation. The key constructs related to positive psychology include character strengths, hope, resilience, optimism and happiness (Chou et al. 2013). According to Seligman and Peterson (2004), Positive psychology has three central concerns: Positive emotions, positive individual traits, and positive institutions. Positive emotions are concerned with being content with one's past, happiness in the present, and having hope for the future. Understanding positive individual traits consists of the study of strengths and virtues, such as the capacity for love and work, courage, compassion, resilience, creativity, curiosity, integrity, self-knowledge, moderation, self-control, and wisdom. Understanding positive institutions requires the study of the strengths that encourage better communities, such as justice, responsibility, civility, parenting, nurturance, work ethics, leadership, team work, purpose, and tolerance. Some researchers in this field suggested that positive psychology can be described into three overlapping areas of research:

1.   **Pleasant life:** The pleasant life or **life of enjoyment** examines how people optimally experience, forecast, and savour the

positive feelings and emotions that are part of normal and healthy living i.e. relationship, hobbies, interests, entertainment, etc. Pleasure is the process of maximizing positive emotion and minimizing negative emotion and is referred to as the pleasant life which involves enjoyable positive experiences.

2. **Good life:** The good life refers to those factors that contribute to most predominantly to a well lived life. Good life, or the **life of engagement** studies the beneficial effects of involvement, pre-occupation, and flow felt by individuals when optimally engaged with their primary activities. Qualities that define good life are those that enrich our lives, make life worth living and foster strong character (Crompton, 2005). According to positive Psychology, the good life must include relationship with other people and the society as a whole. Engagement is the process of being immersed and absorbed in the task at hand and is referred to as the good life which involves being actively involved in life and all that it requires and demands. Thus, the good life is considered to result from the individual cultivating and investing their signature strengths and virtues in their relationships, work, and leisure. Flow is experienced when there is a perfect match between a person's strength and his current task i.e. when one feels confident of accomplishing a chosen or assigned task.

3. **Meaningful life:** The meaningful life or **life of affiliation** questions how individuals derive a positive sense of well-being, belonging, meaning, and purpose from being part of and contributing back to something larger and more permanent than themselves i.e. nature, social groups, organizations, movements, traditions, belief systems, etc. Meaningful life creates a sense of deeper meaning and purpose in life. It produces life regulation qualities that allow us to regulate our day-to-day behaviour in such a way that we can accomplish our goals. Some of these qualities include a sense of individuality

or autonomy, and a high degree of healthy self-control and wisdom to guide behaviour. Meaning is the process of having a higher purpose in life than ourselves and is referred to as the meaningful life which involves using our strengths and personal qualities to serve this higher purpose. The meaningful life like the good life involves the individual applying their signature strengths in activities, but the difference is that these activities are perceived to contribute to the greater benefits in the meaningful life.

We see that positive psychology has many of the features of a new school of thought. Positive psychologists believe happiness can be studied. They are of opinion that happiness comes from meeting challenges, choosing one's own goals, and creating meaning in life. However, positive psychology is not intended to present a complete picture of psychology. In this context Seligman (2002) commented that, "we see positive psychology as a mere change in focus for psychology; from the study of some of the worst things in life to the study of what makes life worth living". Thus, we do not see positive psychology as a replacement for any other streams before, but it can be seen as an enlargement and extension of the prevalent area of psychology. Positive psychology is to build a science that supports:

- Families and schools that allow children to flourish.
- Workplace that foster satisfaction and high productivity.
- Therapists who nurture their patient's strengths.
- Dissemination of positive psychology interventions in schools, organizations, and communities.

To sum up the goals of positive psychology, the definition given by Peterson (2008) needs to be quoted that says, "Positive psychology is the scientific study of what makes life most worth living". To elaborate this brief description a bit further, positive psychology is a scientific approach for studying human thoughts, feelings, and behaviour with a focus on strengths instead of weaknesses; building the good in life instead of repairing the bad, and enhancing the lives of average people up to 'great' instead of focusing solely on those who are struggling to reach up to 'normal'. The plethora of research papers on positive topics has provided a vast storehouse of knowledge on how to encourage ourselves and those around us to live the best lives possible. In general, the greatest prospect of positive psychology is that it guides us to shift our emphasis in the positive direction. A relatively small change in one's outlook can bring significant difference in the well-being and quality of life of the individual.

Pioneers of Positive Psychology

Abraham Maslow's Contribution to Positive Psychology

The term positive psychology was introduced by **Abraham Maslow** who is considered as one of the founders of humanistic psychology. In fact, the term **positive psychology** was first coined by Maslow in his book, **Motivation and personality**. Maslow and other proponents of positive psychology were driven by the idea that traditional psychology has abandoned studying the entire human experience in favour of focusing only on mental illnesses. It was pointed out that psychology is inclined to show our negative side by revealing much about our illnesses and shortcomings, but not enough of our virtues or aspirations (Maslow, 1954). Maslow even used the term Positive Psychology to refer to his brand of humanistic psychology, though modern positive psychologists like Martin Seligman claim that humanistic psychology; lacks adequate empirical validation. To a positive psychologist, optimizing the life and well-being of a person who is healthy is just as important as normalizing the life of a person who is sick, and Maslow helped legitimize this idea within the field of psychology.

Maslow's **humanistic psychology** is based on the belief that people are born with the desire to achieve their maximum potential or reach a point Maslow termed **self-actualization.** Maslow's key concepts include his famous hicrarchy of need theory and his analysis of the characteristics of psychologically healthy people. Maslow believed that humanistic psychology should be based on the study of **healthy and creative individuals**. For this reason, he was interested in studying the lives and patterns of famous people. Humanistic psychologists argued in favour of finding people's strengths instead of focusing on deficiencies. Maslow stated that while Sigmund Freud focused on treating 'sick people', his approach focused on helping people discover positive outcomes or choices.

Maslow's Hierarchy of Needs: The hierarchy of needs comes from Maslow's belief that the fundamental desires of human beings are similar despite the multitude of conscious desires. Maslow describes his hierarchy of needs as being made up of five needs, which are physiological, safety, love, esteem, and self-actualization arranged in a pyramid manner, with physiological needs making up the bottom of the pyramid. Maslow's hierarchy of needs is the framework around which humanistic psychology is built. Like other theories of development, it is a stage-based theory. A person must complete one level of the hierarchy to move on to the next, but not all people may have to move through all stages.

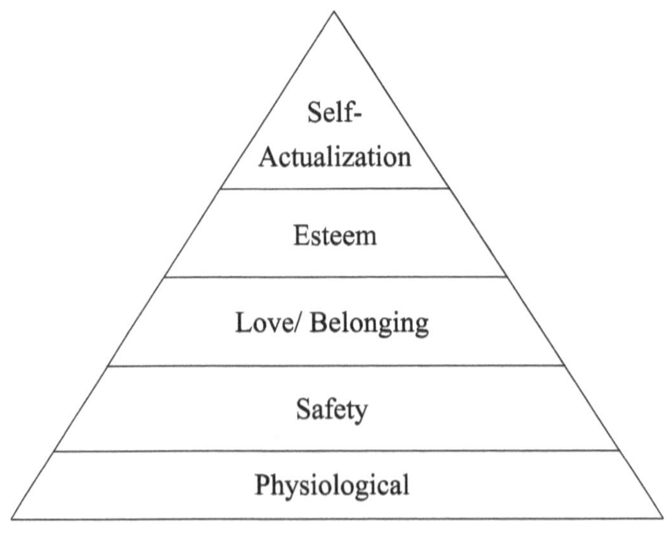

Maslow's Need Hierarchy (1954)

- Basic physiological needs such as food, shelter, and sleep.
- Safety needs such as security, stability, and order.
- Social needs such as love, belonging and friendship.
- Esteem needs include acceptance by others, a sense of achievement, and independence.
- Self-actualization, the innate human tendency towards wholeness and full potential.

In Maslow's need hierarchy, the physiological needs make up the bottom of the pyramid and self-actualization needs occupy the top position of the pyramid. Maslow (1954) assumes that human motives are arranged in a hierarchy of potency. The needs that have the greatest potency at any given time dominate behaviour and demand satisfaction. The individual feels 'driven' by a high priority need. When that need is satisfied, a higher-order motive or class of motives makes it appearance and demands satisfaction, and so on to the top of the hierarchy. If one of these needs is unsatisfied, the individual is dominated by that need. Thus, the hungry individual is dominated by hunger. When the **basic physiological needs** are satisfied, the next higher order of needs emerges and dominates the individual.

Individual seeks **safety or security**. Maslow believes that safety needs are most readily observable in the child because of children's relative helplessness and dependence on adults. The child prefers a predictable, orderly routine; and reacts with feelings of fear and insecurity if confronted with novel, threatening, or terrifying stimuli. Parental quarrels and threats of separation are particularly harmful to a child's sense of well-being. In later years, on the adult level, the individual seeks security by saving money, building a home, and finding a secured job.

Maslow refers to the next higher order of motives as the **belongingness and love needs**. These needs become apparent when the two lower order needs are well satisfied. The individual seeks friends, likes to nurture affectionate relationships, and makes effort for belonging to a group. This belongingness and identification with a particular group adds to his self-identity. The fourth order of needs is esteem needs. These include the desire for a strongly based high evaluation of the self. This **esteem needs** encourage a feeling of worth and adequacy. The individual perceives himself relevant not only to his family but to the society as well. Lack of satisfaction of these needs imbibes discouragement, feelings of inferiority, and worthlessness.

Finally, if all the above needs are satisfied, the need for self-actualization impels the individual to activity. In Maslow's own words, "A musician must make music, an artist must paint, and a poet must write if he is ultimately to be at peace with himself". What a man can be he must be. This need is called **self-actualization**. Maslow again writes self-actualization is not, however, restricted only to the creative characteristics of genius. A fine artist, an athlete, a good workman, may be actualizing their potential abilities in doing well what they can do best.

In later papers Maslow (1971) added two additional classes of needs to his basic theory of motivation. These were the needs for **knowing and understanding** and the **aesthetic needs**. The needs for knowing and understanding may be included under the broad heading of **curiosity**. The aesthetic needs are expressed in the deep-seated need for beauty as promoting a feeling of well-being.

Maslow has distinguished between **growth motivation** and **deficiency motivation**. The self-actualizing tendency is growth motivation. Self-actualization is the goal of human development and occurs when a person meets his/ her full potential. Self-actualized people are joyful, empathetic, giving and fulfilled. Maslow (1971) pointed out that self-actualized people are driven by **meta-motivation.** They do not seek fulfilment of their basic needs; they are driven to fulfil their full potential. Maslow identified two types of cognitions. Associated with deficiency needs is a state of **Deficiency cognition,** sometimes called **D-cognition.** It is a way of thinking that focuses on what one doesn't have and how to get it. **Being-cognition,** by contrast, is a form of thinking for people who are self-actualizing. They focus on acceptance, justice, harmony, simplicity, and similar goals and values. Maslow himself called his work positive psychology rather than humanistic psychology.

Albert Bandura: Bandura is an influential social cognitive psychologist who is best known for his **social learning theory**, the concept of **self-efficacy**. He is a professor Emeritus at Stanford University. The initial phase of Bandura's research analysed the foundations of human learning and the willingness of children and adults to imitate behaviour observed in others, in particular, aggression. He found that according to social learning theory, models are an important source for learning new behaviours and for achieving behavioural change in institutionalized settings. During a period dominated by behaviourism in the idea of Skinner; Bandura believed the role of reward and punishment in classical and operant conditioning were inadequate as a framework, and that much human behaviour were learned from other humans. Bandura began to analyse means of treating unruly aggressive children by identifying sources of violence in their lives. In 1965 Bandura conducted an experiment known as the **Bobo doll experiment**, designed to show that similar behaviours were learned by individuals shaping their own behaviour after the actions of models. In Bobo doll experiment, researchers physically and verbally abused a clown-faced inflatable toy in front of preschool-age children. This led the children to later mimic the behaviour of the adults by attacking the doll in the same fashion. Bandura's results from the experiment changed the course of modern psychology. It helped shifting the focus in academic psychology from pure behaviourism to cognitive psychology. Moreover, the Bobo doll experiment emphasized how young individuals are influenced by the acts of adults.

Bandura made research study on homes in which the father rejects his son or plays a reduced role, and the mother tends to be the dominant parental figure. It was found that there was much higher incidence of theft and personal crime in societies where the family typically restricts opportunities for the young boy to identify with his father. In a study of delinquent and non-delinquent boys, it was found that the great majority of delinquent boys felt rejected by their fathers but loved by their mothers, while the non-delinquents felt loved equally by both parents. In the background of a group of aggressively delinquent boys, Bandura delineated a pattern in which father rejection was combined with inconsistent handling of the boy by both parents. To complicate the pathogenic family picture, the father typically used physically punitive method of discipline, thus increasing the hostility the boy already felt for him. The end result of such a pattern is a hostile, defiant, inadequately socialized boy who lacks normal inner controls and tends to act out his aggressive impulses. As a consequence of paternal rejection, the father may play a reduced role, while the mother plays the dominant role in providing affection, discipline and other socialized behaviours. During adolescence, the youth who has identified with his mother and relied on her as a role model presumably has difficulty shaping a masculine self-concept. As a consequence, he tends to be rebellious and is likely to engage in offensive behaviour to reassure himself of his courage, independence, and masculinity. In another study it was found that the sons perceived their fathers as vague, lacking in warmth and unclear characters where the fathers were unable to discipline their sons and abandoned their roles in child rearing altogether. The mothers were given their due importance and the sons frequently reported having had good relationships with them. By the mid-1980s, Bandura's research had taken a more holistic bent, and his analysis gave a more comprehensive overview of human cognition in the context of social learning. Bandura expanded **social learning theory** to be known as **social cognitive theory.**

Albert Bandura's **self-efficacy theory** originated from his **social-cognitive theory.** It relates to a person's perception of their ability to reach a goal and the belief that one is capable of performing it in a certain way in order to reach them. This concept has been of great importance and use in positive psychology. **Self-efficacy** according to

Bandura is a personal judgment of "how well one can execute courses of action required to deal with prospective situations". Psychologists have studied self-efficacy from several perspectives. Self-belief in innate abilities means valuing one's particular set of cognitive strengths. It also involves determination and perseverance to overcome obstacles that would interfere with utilizing those innate abilities to achieve goals. Self-efficacy affects every area of human endeavour. Bandura felt that unless people believe that they can produce desired effects by their actions, they have little incentives to act or to persevere in the face of difficulties. Whether other factors serve as guides and motivators, they are rooted in the core belief that one has the power to achieve changes by one's actions. Empirical studies support that optimism, positive thinking about the future, hedonic balance with positive affect exceeding negative affect and satisfaction with one's life are rooted in the belief in personal efficacy. Evidence that positive affect raises perceived self-efficacy and negative affect lowers it suggests that the impact of affect on psychosocial functioning works partly through beliefs of personal efficacy. According to Bandura, in everyday life, adaptive functioning requires **regulation of affect**. Perceived self-efficacy to regulate positive and negative affect also plays a role in the quality of psychosocial functioning. Self-efficacy is the belief that we have in our own abilities, specifically our ability to meet the challenges ahead of us and complete a task successfully. General self-efficacy refers to our overall belief in our ability to succeed, but there are many more specific forms of self-efficiency as well.

Self-efficacy and Motivation: Although self-efficacy and motivation are deeply interlinked, they are two separate constructs. Self-efficacy is based on individual's belief in their own capacity to achieve, while motivation is based on the individual's desire to achieve. Those with high self-efficacy often have high motivation and vice versa. However, it is not a predetermined conclusion. Still, it is a fact that when an individual gains self-efficacy through the experience of success; they generally get a boost in motivation to continue learning and making progress. The relationship can also work in the other direction to generate a sort of success cycle; when an individual is highly motivated to learn and succeed, they are more likely to achieve their goals, giving them an experience that contributes to their overall self-efficacy.

Self-efficacy and Resilience: Albert Bandura is known for his social learning theory and the theoretical construct of self-efficacy. While experiences of success certainly makeup a large portion of self-efficacy development, there is also chance for failure. Those with a high level of self-efficacy are not only more likely to succeed, but they are also more likely to bounce back and recover from failure. In order to succeed, people need a sense of self-efficacy, to struggle together with resilience to meet the inevitable obstacles and inequities of life.

Self-efficacy and Confidence: self-efficacy is also positively related to confidence, but these are not the same thing; confidence is a non-descriptive term that refers to strength of belief. Perceived self-efficacy refers to belief in one's capabilities that one can produce given level of attainment. Self-efficacy and confidence can work in a positive cycle; the more confident a person is in his abilities, the more likely he is to succeed, which provides him with experiences to develop his self-efficacy. This high self-efficacy, in turn, gives him more confidence in himself and round it goes.

Self-efficacy and Locus of control: The locus of control refers to where we believe the power to alter our life events resides: within us (internal locus of control) or outside us (external locus of control). It is to be noted that those with high self-efficacy have an internal locus of control.

Self-efficacy and Stress, Depression, and Anxiety: The relationship between self-efficacy and anxiety was initially proposed by Bandura. He noted that low self-efficacy is basically the belief that one does not have control over a situation and cannot manage potential threats, which logically leads to increased anxiety. This can continue as a self-repeating cycle in which low self-efficacy leads to greater anxiety and greater avoidant behaviours, which lead to fewer opportunities to successfully cope with distress, which in turn lowers the individual's self-efficacy even more (Bandura, 1988). In adolescents, low self-efficacy is strongly related to anxiety and neuroticism, anxiety disorder symptoms, and depressive symptoms. Further, those with low self-efficacy were more likely to experience social phobia and panic disorders.

Social Learning theory: Social learning theory describes the acquisition of skills that are developed primarily within a social group. Social learning depends on how individuals either succeed or fail at dynamic interactions within groups, and promotes the development of individual emotional and practical skills as well as accurate perceptions of self and acceptance of others. According to this theory, people learn from one another through **observation, imitation and modelling**. Social learning theory got modified into social cognitive theory that states that models have a great impact on personality development. Children learn to be assertive, conscientious, self-sufficient, dependable, easy-going and so forth by observing others behaving in these ways. Parents, teachers, siblings, and peers serve as models for young children. Bandura and his colleagues have done extensive research showing how models influence the development of aggressiveness, gender roles, and moral standards in children (Bandura, 1973).

Social Cognitive Theory: The social cognitive theory is based on the work of Bandura and he incorporates the idea of self-efficacy. Bandura has defined self-efficacy as one's belief in one's ability to succeed in specific situations or accomplish a task. One's sense of self-efficacy can play a major role in how one approaches goals, and challenges. Social cognitive theory emphasizes the role of observational learning and social experiences in the development of personality. The main concept in social cognitive theory is that an individual's actions and reactions including social behaviours and cognitive processes in almost every situation are influenced by the actions that individuals observe in others. Since self-efficacy is developed from external experiences and self-perception, it is an important aspect of social cognitive theory. According to Bandura's theory, people with high self-efficacy are those who believe they can perform well are more likely to view difficult tasks as something to be mastered rather than seeking opportunities to avoid the same.

Social Cognitive Theory of Self-efficacy is based on six constructs:

- **Reciprocal determinism:** the dynamic interaction of person and behaviour.
- **Behavioural capability:** the individual's actual ability to perform the appropriate behaviour.
- **Observational learning:** learning a new skill or piece of knowledge by observing others.
- **Reinforcements:** the external responses to the individual's behaviour.
- **Expectations:** the anticipated consequences of behaviour.
- **Self-efficacy:** the person's confidence in his /her ability to perform behaviour.

The ultimate goal of social cognitive theory is to explain how people regulate their behaviour through control and reinforcement to achieve goal-directed behaviour that can be mastered over time.

Self-Concept theory: Self-concept theory seeks to explain how people perceive and interpret their own existence from clues they receive from external sources, focusing on how these impressions are organized and how they are active throughout life. Successes and failures are closely related to the ways in which people learned to view themselves and their relationship with others. This theory describes self-concept as learned, organized, and dynamic.

Attribution theory: Attribution theory focuses on how people attribute events and how these beliefs interact with self-perception. The controllability of an attribution is the extent to which the individual can influence it. Attribution theory states three major causes of behaviour and events.

- **Locus** is the location of the perceived cause. When the locus is internal (dispositional), feelings of self-esteem and self-efficacy are to be enhanced by success and diminished by failure.
- **Stability** describes whether the cause is perceived as static or dynamic overtime. It is clearly related to expectations and goals in that when people attribute their failures to stable factors such as the difficulty of a task, they will expect to fail in the future.

Bandura opined that self-efficacy beliefs influence whether people think pessimistically or optimistically i.e. self-enhancing or self-debilitating ways. Efficacy beliefs also shape people's expectations i.e. whether they expect their efforts to produce favourable outcomes or adverse ones. In addition, efficacy beliefs determine how opportunities and impediments are viewed. People with low self-efficacy are easily convinced of the futility of effort in the face of adversities. They are ready to refrain themselves from trying out new options. However, people with high self-efficacy remain resilient to adversities. Efficacy beliefs determine the choices people make at important decisional points. Beliefs in personal efficacy can, therefore, play a vital role in shaping and influencing the types of activities people aspire to accomplish in their life.

How to Improve Self-Efficacy

People's beliefs in their efficacy can be developed in four ways:

- Mastery experiences
- Vicarious experiences
- Verbal persuasion
- Emotional and physiological states

Mastery Experiences: These refer to the experiences we gain when we take up a new challenge and become successful. Success generates a powerful self-efficacy. Failures undermine it; especially in early phases of efficacy development when people are not confident about their capabilities. The most powerful path to self-efficacy is through mastering new skills. Sometimes new skills come easily in case of learning some stereotyped tasks, whereas in acquiring more difficult skills, people usually make mistakes. How they handle these failure experiences is the key to learning self-efficacy. If you give up when you make mistakes, your failure imbibes self-doubts or low self-efficacy. On the contrary, if you persist through failure experiences, you learn the lesson of self-efficacy. 'I can do it' approach certainly provides the mastery experiences needed to build self-efficacy to encounter future challenges and build up confidence. When people experience only success at every opportunity; they always expect positive results. It may so happen that these people are likely to lose their patience and feel depressed when they have to face failures under some circumstances. Hence, resilient efficacy requires overcoming obstacles through persistent effort. Resilience is built up by encountering and managing failures.

Vicarious Experiences: The second way of developing self-efficacy is through vicarious experiences. Vicarious experience is simply having a role model to observe and imitate. Models are sources of aspirations, competencies, and motivation. By observing people similar to oneself succeed by continuous efforts, uplifts observer's beliefs in their own abilities. In contemporary society, ideas, values, belief systems and life styles are socially transmitted in the electronic media. When we have positive role models who display a healthy level of self-efficacy, we are likely to internalize some of these positive beliefs into the self. Hence, selecting successful role models is important; observing unsuccessful ones can undermine self-efficacy.

Verbal Persuasion: The third mode of influence on self-efficacy is verbal persuasion. The verbal persuasion factor describes the positive impact that our words can have on someone's self-efficacy. When people are persuaded to believe in themselves; they exercised more effort. This increases their chances of success. By encouraging and motivating to face any challenge, self-efficacy can also be enhanced.

Finally, we are all aware of the fact that health is an important factor in determining self-efficacy. It is certainly easier to boost self-efficacy when someone is enjoying good health and cheer. Tension, anxiety, and depression are signs of personal deficiencies and reflect poor mental health. Occasionally, mood also affects how people perceive their own self-efficacy. Positive mood reports a sense of high self-efficacy while a depressed mood reflects a low efficacy level. Thus, efficacy beliefs can be strengthened by enriching and nurturing good mental health.

Carol Dweck: Carol Dweck's work has primarily centred on the psychology of people's motivation, personality, and development. Dweck is a psychologist who has done extensive research over the last thirty years on the cause and effect of how one's thoughts drive them into success or inadequacy. Her book "**Mind-Set: The New Psychology of Success**" explains why intelligence and talent do not automatically bring success. She is one of the leading motivational researchers whose written works and lectures have inspired to find success using positive ideas about what motivates us. Her main contribution to psychology relates to challenging certain aspects of the main theories of intelligence and its implications for success in life. Her book, **Self-theories**: **Their role in motivation, personality, and development**" was awarded book of the year in 1999 by the World Education Federation.

Carol Dweck is considered a pioneering figure in the study of **human motivation.** She is perhaps best known for her research on implicit theories of intelligence and how mind-sets influence motivation and success. There are two main mind-sets we can navigate life with: **growth and fixed**. Having a growth mind-set is essential for success. With **fixed mind-set** we believe that our qualities are unchangeable and we want to prove ourselves correct over and over by sticking to our old habits, rather than learning from our mistakes. Thus, the fixed mind-set can negatively impact all aspects of our life. Ideas about risk and effort come from our mind-set. Some people realize the value of challenging themselves by taking personal risks and striving for greater goals. According to

Dweck, people who hold an innate view of intelligence, or believe that talent and ability are inborn traits; possess a **fixed mind-set**. Those who believe that intelligence, talent, and abilities can be improved through efforts hold **growth mind-set**. Such mind-sets can play a role in how people tackle challenges and whether they persist in the face of setbacks. Her work reveals that these mind-sets can have a powerful influence on performance and how people deal with challenges according to Dweck (2006), "If parents want to give their children a gift, the best thing they can do is to teach their children to love challenges, be intrigued by mistakes, enjoy efforts, and keep on learning". That way, their children don't become slaves to others' praise. They have a lifelong way to build and repair their own confidence. Dweck's work shows the power of our basic beliefs. Whether conscious or subconscious, they strongly affect what we want and whether we succeed in getting it. Much of what we think we understand of our personality comes from our 'Mind-set'. Dweck writes: What are the consequences of thinking that your intelligence or personality is something you can develop, as opposed to something that is a fixed, deep-seated trait? The outcome of such thinking is the belief that one's intelligence can be grown or developed with persistence, dedication and hard work. Your view of yourself can determine everything. The passion for stretching yourself and sticking to it is the hallmark of growth mind-set. This is the mind-set that allows people to thrive during some of the most challenging times in their lives. Dweck writes, "In the growth mind-set, failure can be a painful experience. But it does not define you. It is a problem to be faced, dealt with and we can learn so many things from such failure". This view creates a love of learning and a resilience that is essential for great accomplishment.

According to Briggs growth mind-set can be developed in the following ways:

- Acknowledge and embrace imperfections.
- View challenges as opportunities.

- Try different learning tactics.
- Follow the research on brain plasticity; since the brain is not fixed; the mind should not be either.
- Replace the word 'failing' with the word 'learning'.
- Stop seeking approval.
- Value the process over the end result.
- Cultivate a sense of purpose.
- Celebrate growth with others.
- Emphasize growth over speed.
- Reward actions, not traits.
- Redefine 'genius'.
- Portray criticism as positive.
- Disassociate improvement from failure.
- Provide regular opportunities for reflection.
- Place effort before talent.
- Highlight the relationship between learning and 'brain training'.
- Cultivate grit.
- Abandon the image.
- Use the word 'yet'.
- Learning from other people's mistakes.
- Make a new goal for every goal accomplished.
- Take risks in the company of others.
- Think realistically about time and effort.
- Take ownership over your attitude.

All these above mentioned tips are helpful for cultivating growth mind-set. Once we develop a growth mind-set, we should own it. We must acknowledge and appreciate ourselves for possessing a growth mentality and consciously wish that the growth mind-set guides us at every step of our life.

To summarize, it can be said that a fixed mind-set in this scenario is convincing to oneself that things won't go well under any circumstances. A growth mind-set, on the other hand, is having the belief that we may make mistakes; however, it is an opportunity for us to learn. People with a growth mind-set are perpetually learning and improving. They face challenges, grow from failure, value constructive criticisms, and learn from others' success. People with a fixed mind-set believe that they are either born good at something or they are not. This leads them not to work hard, give up more easily, and reject constructive criticisms. According to growth mind-set, success is a direct result of effort and hard work. Dweck's explanation and importance of growth mind-set can be practically realized when it comes to achievement and success at every aspect of life.

Contribution of Martin Seligman to Positive Psychology

Martin Seligman is a researcher with a broad range of experience in psychology. He is a leading authority in the fields of positive **psychology, resilience, learned helplessness, depression, optimism, and pessimism.** He is also a recognized authority on interventions that prevent depression, and building strengths and well-being. Seligman served as the Director of Positive Psychology Centre at the University of Pennsylvania. He is the author of around 20 self-help books and more than 250 articles about the science of what makes life worth living. Seligman is also the founder of the positive psychology centre at the University of Pennsylvania. The mission of this centre is to promote research, training education, and the dissemination of positive psychology.

Seligman's research in the 1960s and 70s laid the foundation for the well-known psychological theory of **learned helplessness.** This theory explains how humans and animals can learn to become helpless and feel they have lost control over what happens to them. Seligman connected this phenomenon with depression, noting that many people suffering from depression feel helpless as well. His work on the subject provided inspiration, ideas, and evidence to back up many treatments for depressive symptoms as well as strategies for preventing depression. Seligman realized that he had more to offer and in particular he was determined to do more work on the positive, the uplifting, and the inspiring. **Learned helplessness** is a term specifying an organism learning to accept and endure unpleasant stimuli, and unwilling to avoid them, even when it is avoidable. The idea behind the theory of learned helplessness is that we can be conditioned to think that we have no control over the outcome of a situation even when we actually do have the power to help ourselves. This occurs when we are repeatedly presented with an aversive stimulus. People think that they can neither change a situation nor miss opportunities that make them feel helpless. In the process, people are more likely to develop a mental illness such as **clinical depression**. After making a name for him with learned helplessness, Seligman turned his attention to other traits, characteristics, and perspectives that could be learned. He was not satisfied with psychology's focus on the negatives since much attention was given to mental illness, trauma, suffering and pain and there was little attention on happiness, well-being, strengths, and flourishing. Seligman was elected as the President of the American Psychological Association in 1998 and the central theme he chose for his term as president was positive psychology. He proposed a new subfield of psychology with a focus on what is **life-giving** rather than **life-exhausting**. Seligman viewed **mental health** to be more than just the **absence of illness** and began a new era that focused on what makes people happy and fulfilled. He believed that a psychology of positive human functioning will arise and achieve a scientific understanding and effective interventions to build thriving in individuals, families, and communities. It is a matter of great satisfaction that over the last twenty years, general interest in positive psychology has grown tremendously. Of late, more and more people are searching for information on how they can become more fulfilled and achieve their full potential. Seligman (2002) distinguished between four levels of analysis for positive psychology.

Four Levels of Analysis for Positive Psychology

+ The **wellsprings of interest** to positive psychology may be defined as the precursors and facilitators of the processes and mechanisms. They include subjects like the genetic foundations of well-being and the early environmental experiences that allow the development of strengths and virtues.

+ The **processes of interest** to positive psychology may be defined as those psychological components that lead to a good life. Positive psychology should seek to understand the factors that facilitate optimal functioning.

+ The **mechanisms of interest** to positive psychology may be defined as those extra psychological factors that facilitate the pursuit of a good life. For example, these mechanisms may be personal and social relationships, working environments, organization and institutions, communities, and the broad social, cultural, political, and economic systems in which our lives are completely implanted.

+ The **outcomes of interest** to positive psychology may be defined as those subjective, social and cultural states that characterize a good life. At individual level factors like happiness, well-being, fulfilment, and health; positive communities and institutions that foster good lives at the interpersonal level, and political, economic, and environmental policies that promote harmony and sustainability at the social level.

Seligman's PERMA Model

Seligman proposed PERMA model which is widely recognized and influential model in positive psychology. This model has very clearly explained and defined well-being in greater depth. PERMA is an abbreviation for the five facts of well-being. According to Seligman:-

- **P- Positive Emotions:** By seeking positive emotion alone is not a very effective way to boost our well-being, however, experiencing positive emotion is still an important factor. Part of well-being is enjoying yourself in the moment i.e. experiencing positive emotions.

- **E- Engagement:** Having a sense of enjoyment in which we may become completely absorbed in something we enjoy and excel at. It is difficult to develop a sense of well-being without being engaged and involved in it.

- **R- Relationship:** we are all social creatures, and we rely on connection with others to flourish. Deep, meaningful and genuine relationships with others are vital to our well-being.

- **M- Meaning:** Even who are happy most of the time may not have a developed sense of well-being if they do not find meaning in their life. When we dedicate ourselves to a cause or recognize something bigger than ourselves; we experience a sense of meaning.

- **A- Accomplishment:** We all thrive when we are succeeding achieving our goals, and improving ourselves. As Seligman stated without a drive to accomplish and achieve, we are missing one of the puzzle pieces of authentic well-being.

This model gives us a comprehensive framework for understanding well-being as well as a foundation for improving well-being. When you are looking to enhance your own sense of authentic happiness and well-being, all you need to do is to take care of the following aspects:

- **Experiencing more positive emotions**, do more of the things that make you happy, and bring enjoyment into your daily routine.

- **Working on your engagement**, pursue hobbies that interest you, develop your skills, and look for a job more suited to your passions. When there is consonance between passions and professions people enjoy job satisfaction.

- **Improve the quality of your relationships with others,** work on building more positive and supportive relationships with your friends, family, and significant others.

- **Seek out meaning** when you do not find your work meaningful, look for it in volunteering opportunities, personal hobbies or leisure activities, or acting as a mentor for others.
- **Keep your focus on achieving your goals,** but don't stress yourself too much; try to keep your ambitions in balance with all other important things in life.

The five aspects of PERMA model discussed above are measurable, and are also important for an overall sense of well-being. Positive emotions are important and are part of PERMA model; however, focusing just on positive emotions will not help you to develop a comprehensive sense of well-being, including engagement, meaning, success, and positive relationships with others.

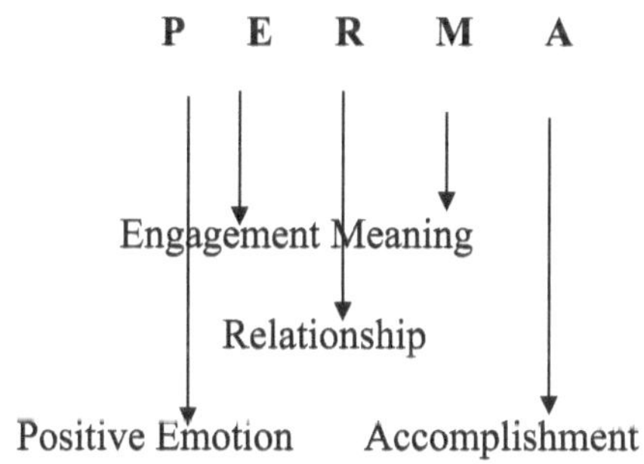

Introducing a New Theory of Well-Being

Flourishing: Product of Pursuit and Engagement

Flourishing refers to the state when we are concerned and merged with each aspect of the **PERMA** model and build up a solid **sense of well-being**. It is not only rising to the occasion but being raised by it. We flourish when we cultivate our talents and strengths, develop deep and meaningful relationships, feel pleasure and enjoyment, and make a meaningful contribution to the world. We flourish when we find fulfilment in life along with achieving more traditional objectives related to success and when we are truly living the good life (Seligman,

2011). Flourishing is the product of pursuit and engagement of an authentic life that brings inner joy and happiness in achieving goals, being connected with life passions, and relishing accomplishments through the peaks and valleys of life. It is to be noted that **flourishing is not a trait, a characteristic; flourishing is a process that requires action**. Truly, it does not come easily; however, it is possible that anyone can flourish. Positive psychology is intended to help us savour 'living' rather than 'just survive' in a stressful world.

Seligman's Manual on Character Strengths and Virtues

Seligman worked on a classification manual called the **character strengths and virtues** that focuses on what can go right instead of what can go wrong. This classification manual of character strengths and virtues consists of six classes of virtues that include 24 character strengths. The manual functions as the Positive counterpart to the **Diagnostic and statistical Manual of Mental Disorders (DSM)**, which studies the insanities. Seligman's character strength offers a review of the traits that influence well-being and sanity. It is true that all cultures around the world have emphasized the study of human strengths and virtues. While human virtues are always valued, different cultures express or act on virtues in different ways based on differing societal values and norms. Positive psychologists take keen interest in identifying human strengths and encourage individuals to nurture these traits to maintain well-being. The **Aristotelian Model** focuses on the virtuous individual and his inner traits, dispositions, and motives that qualify him to be virtuous. Moreover, in the Aristotelian Model, the virtues of the soul are of two types: virtue of thought and virtue of character. **Virtue of thought** arises and grows mostly from teaching i.e. it needs experience and time. **Virtue of character** results from following the right habits. Hence, it is accepted that none of the virtues of character arise in us naturally. We all know that the concept of good character constitutes one of the conceptual cornerstones of positive psychology. Moreover, for positive psychology, **Wisdom, courage, humanity, justice, temperance, and transcendence** are categories of virtue, which are postulated to be **universal virtues** (Seligman, 2002). Further. The individual normally undergoes continuous development or growth towards realization of the given virtue potentials. Seligman differentiates between strengths and talents as they are often confused in the identification of individual signature strengths. It is suggested that **strengths are moral traits while talents are innate.** Talents are said to be relatively automatic whereas strengths are more voluntary. Although, talent does not involve a choice about possessing it; there is a choice of whether to develop and make use of it. According to Seligman strength involves choices about when to use it and whether to keep building it. It is emphasized that these character strengths exist on a continuum. Positive traits are regarded as individual differences that exist in degrees rather than all-or-nothing categories. It is argued that signature strengths are built from the strengths that an individual already possess. The main criteria for character strengths are that each trait should:

- Be stable across time and situations.
- Be valued in its own right, even in the absence of other benefits.
- Be recognized and valued in almost every culture, be considered non-controversial and independent of politics.
- Cultures provide role models that possess the trait so that other people can recognize its worth.

Character strengths are the positive aspects of our personality that affect how we think, feel, and behave. These character strengths are the foundation of positivity in human beings. These are a collection of positive traits that show people's strengths. Character strengths improve our interpersonal relationships. It enhances health and overall well-being. Seligman and his colleagues considered six classes of virtues that are made up of 24 character strengths.

1. **Virtue of Wisdom and Knowledge:** Strengths that accompany this virtue involve acquiring and using knowledge and the underlying character strengths are:

   - **Creativity-** New and original ways to think and do work.
   - **Curiosity-** Exploration and discovery.
   - **Open-Mindedness-** Consider new ideas and try new things. Examine things from all sides and do not jump into conclusions.
   - **Love of learning-** Master new skills and topics of your own interests.
   - **Perspective & Wisdom-** Appreciate that people see things in different ways. Possess the ability to understand the world from multiple points of view.

2. **Virtue of courage:** The braver and more persistent we become, our integrity increases accordingly. We reach a state of feeling energetic. Strengths that accompany this virtue are:

   - **Bravery** – Act with confidence.
   - **Persistence-** Complete what you have started despite obstacles; you never give up.
   - **Integrity-** Present yourself genuinely and sincerely.
   - **Vitality** – Energetic, work with spiritedness.

3. **Virtue of Humanity**: Strengths that accompany this virtue include.

   - **Love** – Value close relationships with others and being close to people.
   - **Kindness-** Being generous to others and enjoying doing good deeds for other people.
   - **Social intelligence-** Aware of other people's thoughts and feelings.

4. **Virtue of Justice:** Strengths that accompany this virtue include those that build a healthy and stable community.

- Being an active citizen who is socially responsible, loyal, and a team member.
- Fairness- Approach situations with an unbiased mind-set and treat everyone with respect.
- Leadership- Value each member of the group and inspire people to do their best.

5. **Virtue of Temperance:**Strengths that are included in this virtue are moderation and self-restraint.

- Forgiveness and mercy - Accept that people make mistakes.
- Humility and modesty – Humbleness, lack of vanity.
- Prudence – Plan for the future and achieve goals by making careful everyday choices.
- Self-Regulation and Self-control – Ability to control emotions and behaviours.

6. **Virtue of Transcendence:** Strengths that accompany this virtue include those that build up connections to the larger universe.

- Appreciation of beauty and excellence- Notice and value the world's beauty.
- Gratitude- Aware of and thankful for good things that happen.
- Hope- Anticipation
- Humour and playfulness- Like to laugh and bring smiles to other people.
- Spirituality – Divine feeling.

Since these virtues are considered too abstract to be studied scientifically, positive psychologists focused their attention on the strengths of character created by virtues and prepared tools for their measurement. The main assessment instruments they used to measure these strengths are:

- Structured interviews
- Questionnaires

- Informant Reports
- Behavioural Experiments
- Observations

In a study on **gender differences and character strengths**, women scored highest on the strengths of honesty, kindness, love, gratitude, and fairness. Femininity is positively correlated with love, social intelligence, and appreciation of beauty, love of learning, forgiveness, spirituality, and creativity. The more masculine a man is, the more he correlated negatively with these characteristics. It is found that men score highest on honesty, hope, humour, gratitude, and curiosity. Men not only scored higher in creativity, but also scored higher in leadership, self-control, and zest. Men also saw strengths such as teamwork, kindness, and courage to be a stronger connection to life satisfaction than other strengths.

Principles of Character Strengths: Character strengths and Virtues (CSV) is a book by Peterson and Seligman (2004) that attempts to present a measure of humanist ideals of virtue in an empirical scientific manner. They stated that character strengths are manifested in our thoughts, emotions, and our behaviour. It is explained that the 24 character strengths are evident in the most widely influential traditions and all cultures of the world. Ranging from bravery and forgiveness to integrity and gratitude, these character strengths are the foundation of the **positivity project's Model**. Making children aware that every one of them has all 24 character strengths provides the foundation for genuine self-confidence grounded in self-awareness. At the same time, it helps children better understand why everyone is different and how to appreciate these differences.

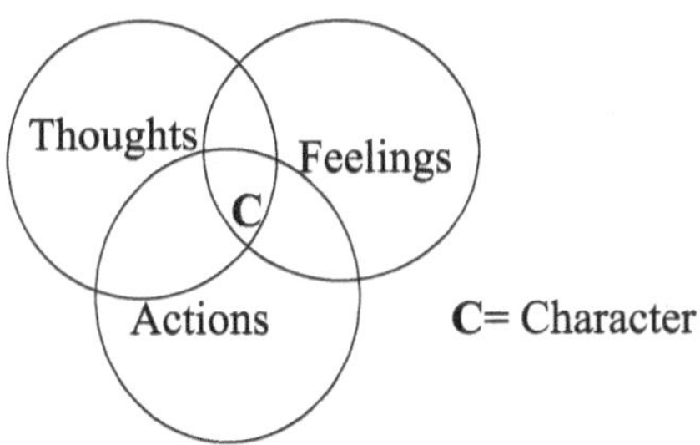

Interaction of Thoughts, Feelings and Actions

Character strengths are not meant for ignoring the negatives; on the other hand, they help us overcome life's inevitable adversities. For example, you cannot be brave without first feeling fear, you cannot show perseverance without first planning to quit, and you cannot show self-control without first being attracted to do something which is not desirable. Peterson and Seligman (2004) theorized that it is natural that children demonstrate gratitude, open mindedness, authenticity, and forgiveness. Park and Peterson's study (2006) confirmed this theoretical speculation, concluding that these character strengths usually require a degree of cognitive maturation that develops during adolescence. Therefore, although gratitude is associated with happiness in adolescents and adulthood; this is not the case in children. The strengths of love, zest, and hope are associated with happiness starting at a very young age. The strengths of love and hope are dependent on the infant and caregiver relationship. A secure attachment to the caregiver at infancy is more likely to result in psychological and social well adjustment throughout their lives. The nurturing of a child plays a significant role in their personality development. Role modelling is an important way of teaching a child certain character strengths as they imitate behaviour and can then internalize the strength as their own. Children may not have the cognitive maturity to display gratitude but have the ability to display love and hope. Gratitude is not expected from a young child but can be taught in later years. Self-theorists have described the child's development as a creative process facilitated by parental acceptance and love. Character strengths are influenced by family, community, societal, and other contextual factors. Moreover, character strengths can be shaped through teaching and acquired through practice.

There are certain character strengths in adolescents that have a strong impact on psychological well-being. These strengths must be nurtured to ensure life -long fulfilment and satisfaction. Adolescents with higher levels of **zest, hope and leadership** displayed lower levels of **anxiety** and **depression** in comparison to their peers with lower levels of these strengths. Positive psychologists stated that character strengths are manifested in our thoughts, emotions, and our behaviour. There are ten principles emerging from the science of character:

1. **Character is plural:** Peterson coined this sentence that has become an axiom in positive psychology. This expands one-dimensional thinking that character means only honesty or integrity. People are not simply kind and respectful, brave and hopeful, or wise and fair. An individual's character is better understood as a unique description of strengths with varying highs and lows.

2. **Character strengths are stable but can and do change:** Character strengths are part of our personality, which we know are relatively stable. At the same time, our character strengths can change based on predictable life events such as starting a family, and unpredictable life events such as trauma and untimely death of somebody close to our heart.

3. **Character strengths are essential:** Character strengths are the basic building blocks of goodness in the individual. They are our true essence; the core parts of our personality that account for being our best selves.

4. **Character strengths can be measured:** The measurement is dimensional, not-categorical. We do not either have a character strength such as creativity or not have it; rather we have degrees of creativity, fitness, zest, and so on.

5. **Character strengths are expressed in degree:** Individuals are likely to express their character strengths in different ways and to a greater extent based on situation. The degree of kindness and love the person expresses may differ depending on the personality of the other family members present and their behaviour towards him. Moreover, the situations like a funeral home, a cinema hall, or a public park will also affect the way the character strength is expressed.

6. **Character strengths are interdependent:** It is difficult to be creative without some level of curiosity, or to be kind without some amount of selflessness. It is likely that in any situation, individuals will express a combination of character strengths, rather than one character strength alone. In a given situation, interactions among strength may highlight the expression of some strengths while the expression of some other strengths remains unnoticed.

7. **Character strengths can be developed:** Character can be affected through conscious intervention. People can learn to be more curious, more grateful, fairer or more open-minded. The key is practice to break old habits and form new ones.

8. **Character strengths can be overused, misused, or underused:** Character strengths can be expressed in unbalanced or harmful ways i.e. misuse of creativity, overuse of curiosity, and underuse of fairness in judgement.

9. **Character strengths have important consequences:** The outcome of expressing one's character strengths, especially one's signature strengths are connected to many benefits such as increased happiness. Each character strength has unique consequences. Determination seems to be linked with achievement more than most character strengths.

10. **Character strengths are universal:** Character strengths are shared by people with differing beliefs, religious affiliations, and political choices. This makes the application of character

strengths more a matter of synthesis i.e. gathering and bridging what is best in us.

Seligman opined that the top five of a group of 24 widely recognized positive characteristics as **signature strengths.** These characteristics are deeply rooted in all and express themselves in six universally recognized human virtues: **Wisdom, courage, justice, humanity, temperance, and spirituality**. In order to enjoy the high levels of satisfaction associated with the **Good Life,** it is suggested that you need to:

- Identify your main signature strengths.
- Assess which ones you are actually using on a regular basis and which ones are neglected.
- Re-craft your work, friendships, and leisure and use your main strengths.

By utilizing the signature strengths and capabilities on regular basis, one can achieve a profound sense of well-being. Hence, we can have the privilege of enjoying **flow** state when we give our hundred percent that results complete absorption in what we are doing.

Positive Emotions

We know the mission of positive psychology is to understand and promote the factors that allow individuals, communities, and societies to flourish. What role do positive emotions play in this mission? The answer seems simple at the outset: **Positive emotions** serve as indicators of **flourishing, or optimal well-being**. It is a natural consequence that those whose lives are characterized by positive emotions like joy, interest, contentment, love, etc. are not likely to be affected by negative emotions such as anxiety, sadness, anger, and despair. Positive emotions produce flourishing not only in the present pleasant moment but over the long term as well. How do positive emotions contribute to happiness? Fredrickson (2000) realized that joy is an emotion often experienced while playing and that it leads to approaching behaviour. Through play kids enjoy physical, intellectual, social activities and verbal communications as well. Play also encourages curiosity and exploration which are the basis for personal growth and contentment. Hence, feelings of contentment generate flexibility in behaviour and enhance self-confidence which is a pre-requisite for better social skills. Every passion, every emotion, has its effect upon the mind. Every change of mind, however slight, has its effect upon the body.

Happiness is a central concept in our life though we do not know what happiness is and why we strive so tirelessly to attain it. Whether we search for it within ourselves or from external sources; we are all obsessed with the quest for happiness. In fact, when we are close to both extremes of human emotion, i.e. ecstasy and despair; we find absolute fact about what it is in this life that brings us joy or pain. It is no wonder that positive psychology has become popular since it is intended to the scientific study of happiness and other positive experiences in life. To understand happiness, we need to review emotions. The word **emotion** comes from the same root as motion, conveying the idea that emotions move through us and perhaps drive us. Emotions involve not only subjective feelings but also characteristic patterns of physiological arousal, thoughts, and behaviours. Fredrickson (1998) defines emotions as, **multi-component response tendencies that unfold over relatively short time spans.** Psychologists explore the ambiguous descriptions and meanings of 'emotion' who have defined emotion as, **any mental experience with high intensity and high hedonic content (pleasure/ displeasure).** Anger, joy, interest, fear, excitement, and jealousy are some of the common emotions experienced by all of us. Thus, emotions are complex mental responses to stimuli, with an all-embracing disposition that leans towards the positive or the negative. Fredrickson pointed out that positive emotions like joy, interest, contentment, and should be looked at in their own right. Positive emotions not only feel different but function differently. To understand the role of positive emotions, broaden-and-build theory of Fredrickson may be discussed in detail.

Broaden – and – Build theory of Fredrickson

Fredrickson theory states that positive emotions have a broadening effect on the momentary thought action repertoire. They allow us to discard automatic response and encourage looking for creative, flexible, and unpredictable new ways of thinking and acting. By broadening our perspectives and actions, we tend to build important and lasting physical, intellectual, psychological, and social resources. Moreover, positive emotions may allow for more creative cognitive processing, including making more connections. In doing so, the theory provides a new perspective on the evolved adaptive significance of positive emotions. This is the broadening part of the theory. One implication for the broadening hypothesis is that positive emotions may help us process the residue of negative emotions. When negative emotions narrow the momentary thought action repertoire and positive emotions broaden this same repertoire, then positive emotions can function as efficient antidotes for the lingering effects of negative emotions. In other words, positive emotions might correct or undo the after-effects of negative emotions. The ability to cultivate positive emotions is, thus, an important skill for regulating negative emotions. For instance, when your heart rate rises after experiencing a negative emotion, you bounce back to a peaceful pace to experience positive emotions. As Fredrickson (2000) remarks, "the psychological broadening sparked by positive emotions can increase an individual's receptiveness to subsequent pleasant or meaningful events". It implies that positive emotions help in protecting physical health and well-being by correcting or undoing the after effects of negative emotions. If we are keen on improving our quality of life and increase our awareness, then we have to regulate ourselves with positive emotions. We can say that positive emotions fall within a range of pleasure content and evoke a specific positive feeling.

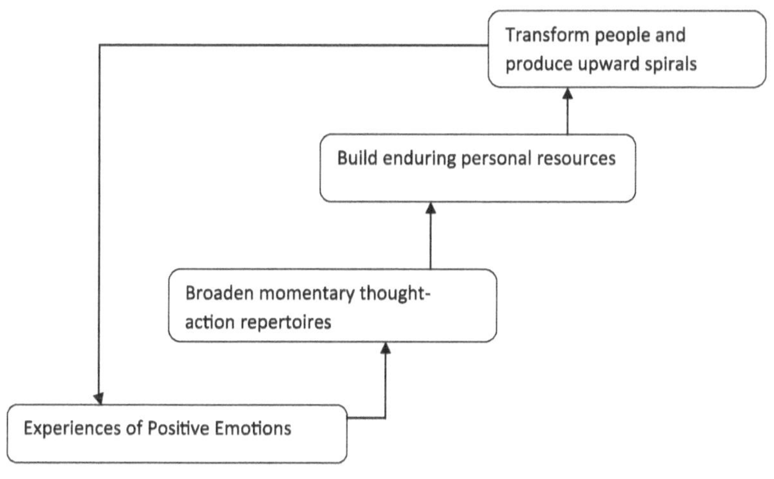

Positive Emotions

Source: **Fredrickson (2002)**

Fredrickson views positive emotions as good feelings that indicate human flourishing. She has outlined the most commonly experienced positive emotions: such as joy, gratitude, serenity, interest, hope, pride, amusement, inspiration, awe and love. These emotions are likely to be perceived as advantageous and desirable emotions to experience. It is advantageous to experience positive emotions because they lead us to engage in activities that add to our behavioural and cognitive repertoires.

The benefits gained from positive emotions have been discussed in the following paragraphs.

Positive Emotions Help us grow: Positive and negative emotions play different roles in individual processing and personal development. Fredrickson (2001) conceptualized that positive emotions broaden people's thought-action repertoire and enable the effective building of skills and resources. These include physical, intellectual, social, and psychological resources. According to her research, positive emotions are internal signals that encourage approach behaviour among us; thus, motivating individuals to engage in their environments and explore novel people, ideas, and situations. When people are open to new ideas and actions, they broaden their horizons, learn, and grow as individuals. Positive emotions both lead to and result from broad-minded coping. The calm and peaceful mind can increase cognitive flexibility and results in a deeper capacity for finding meaning and engaging with life. Studies show that positive emotions improve relationships, therapy, and counselling. These also help in individual development and fulfilment of achievement motivation of the individual. Positive emotions enable us to reach out and connect with others, thereby building stronger bonds. It is a simple fact that when we are in a positive mood, we are more creative and come-up with solutions to problems more effectively than when we are in a negative or neutral mood. Experiencing positive emotions can lead to upward spirals because the openness leads to greater positive emotions, which in turn lead to more openness. So, by broadening people's mind-sets, positive emotions build durable personal resources that function as reserves to be utilized at the time of need of the individual. The broaden-and-build theory views that feeling good can broaden attention, making people more creative and flexible, which help to build other positive personal resources like resilience and optimal functioning.

Health Benefits of Positive Emotions: Positive emotion has direct, positive consequences on physical health. It is related to longevity. When people experience a positive feeling, their immune function improves and their bodies become more capable of fighting off infections. There is increasing evidence that positive emotion makes a unique contribution to heart health. Researchers have found that among the many health benefits of positive emotions; reduction in stress and a boost to general well-being are very important. It is confirmed that experiencing positive emotions helps in modulating reaction to stress and recover from the negative effects of stress more quickly. Experiencing positive emotions may also encourage individuals to make healthier decisions, indirectly contributing to better health. It is observed from research findings that different positive emotions lead to different positive outcomes; for instance, happiness leads to increased risk and enhanced gain focused behaviour, while contentment leads to increased risk avoidance and less focused behaviour. Evidence for the undoing effect of positive emotions suggests that people improve their physical health by cultivating experiences of positive emotions to cope with negative emotions. Positive emotions foster physical health. Negative emotions with their heightened and often prolonged cardiovascular activation have been connected to coronary heart disease. When positive emotions shorten the duration of negative emotional arousal, then only incremental progression towards disease may be slowed down. Relaxation techniques are known to reduce blood pressure in hypertensive adults because they capitalize on the broadening and undoing effects of contentment. Positive emotions have got positive impact on our brain in multiple ways. These benefits are given below:

- Positive emotions increase our performance on a cognitive task by lifting our spirits without distracting us like negative emotions do.
- Positive emotions activate the reward pathways in the brain, contributing to lower levels of stress hormone and greater well-being.
- Positive emotions may help us broaden our horizon and widen our brain's scope of focus.

Fredrickson (2001) reported that positive emotions can have an undoing effect on negative emotions, even to the point of improving physical health as well.

Positive Emotions Facilitate Psychological Well-Being

According to Fredrickson (2004) experiencing positive emotions affects our cognition in two major ways: Positive emotions broaden our conceptualization of a given situation, expanding our ideas and potential actions; build our network of resources by encouraging the development and utilization of strengths, abilities, and reserves. The broaden-and-build theory posits that positive emotions facilitate problem-solving through enhanced creativity, since we tend to view a greater range of possibilities while experiencing positive emotions as compared to negative emotions. In addition to broadening one's mind-set, positive emotions facilitate build and utilize valuable resources to achieve positive outcomes. We can say that experiencing the emotion of hope during difficult times may inspire one to think and act with patience. People with more of positive emotions use resources such as optimism, self-efficiency, resilience, and an active coping style and manage their assigned duties and roles in an effective manner. It is perceived that past is always beautiful since one never realizes any emotion at that time. Emotion builds up at a later stage. Thus, we do not have complete emotions about the present, only about the past. Positive emotions have long been associated with psychological health because they contribute to **positive coping**. Some coping modes suggest that positively coping with life circumstances leads to positive effects. Experiencing positive emotion is, in itself, a coping strategy. Positive emotions are also good for individual exploration, allowing individuals to gather new experiences that facilitate learning. Positive emotions can also help in effective coping behaviour which uplifts mental health. In addition, being focused on a particular goal and by savouring positive emotions, we can save ourselves from depression while boosting our psychological well-being and life satisfaction. Several studies found that well-being is significantly related to good cardiovascular functioning, general health, and overall longevity. Hence, persons while experiencing positive emotions like joy, gratitude, hope or peace cannot experience fear, anger, or sadness at that particular moment. Positive emotions also improve coping and produce well-being. They do so not just in the present pleasant moment, but over the long term as well. Positive emotions can also have profound social and organizational repercussions. Hence, positive emotions are worth cultivating, not just as end states in themselves but also as a means to achieve psychological growth and improved well-being overtime. Evidence for the undoing effect of positive emotions suggests that people might improve their psychological well-being and their physical health by cultivating experiences of positive emotions to counter the effect of negative emotions.

Positive social engagement can improve one's mental and physical health. The expression of positive energy creates a reciprocal response in the other person and the happiness is perpetuated. Studies indicate that social activities, volunteering and other altruistic behaviours are strong sources of positive emotion. Undoubtedly, experiencing pleasure and positive emotion in the moment is important in day-to-day well-being.

Positive Emotions Foster Resilience and Memory: Studies indicate that resilience improves the effectiveness of emotional regulation. It helps the individual to bounce back from stressful events and find meaning in negative experiences. In addition to promoting good physical and psychological health, positive emotions have been found to relate to both resilience and memory. It is found that positive emotions and resilience are positively correlated implying that one influences the other. According to Lazarus (1993) and Carver (1998) resilient individuals are said to bounce back from stressful experiences quickly and efficiently; just as resilient metals bend but do not break. Positive emotions accelerate recovery from negative emotions and they also propel resilient coping. Resilient people experience more positive emotions in the midst of adversity compared to those who are less resilient. Research findings reflect that positive emotions that foster resilience result in improved social skills and higher rates of empathy, cooperation, assertiveness, and self-control among school children.

Application of Broaden-and-Build Theory in the work place: The broaden-and-build theory was developed to explain the role of positive emotions in general. The findings can be applied to organizational behaviour in a very workable way. Emotion is more powerful than reason. Emotion is the driving force behind thinking and reasoning. Emotional intelligence increases the mind's ability to make positive and brilliant decisions in the organization. Workplaces where employees enjoy more of positive emotions are more committed towards their job assignments and there is greater cooperation and team spirit among them. Positive emotions can be encouraged in the following ways among the employees.

Fostering a continuous learning culture: Most organizations prefer their employees to learn and develop their skill sets. This helps the employees to deal with greater complexity and challenges encountered in the process of their work. There can be no transforming of darkness into light and of apathy into movement without emotion. By creating a congenial environment and work culture and encouraging employees to experiment without any apprehension of failure, the positive emotion of **interest** can be cultivated in them. Moreover, inspirational leaders may be invited at regular intervals to address the employees to activate the **intrinsic motivation** and creativity among the employees. It is found that positivity at work leads to enhanced self-efficiency, which in turn, positively affects job satisfaction and mental health. Organizations spend a lot of time and effort on employees' engagement surveys. These surveys provide opportunities for employees to assess their workplace, allowing organizations to focus their efforts on improving employee experience, enhancing productivity and increasing loyalty to the organizations.

Enhancing Employee Engagement Positive emotions have been shown to have a positive impact on relationships in the personal as well as professional life. Emotions and personal life do have an impact on our work. All emotions are positive which gather you and lift you up. Positive emotions have led to enhancements and improvement in work life, physical and mental health, social relationships and community involvement; all of which are either directly or indirectly related to work. Positive emotions contribute to increased self-efficacy, higher job satisfaction, and better mental health. Positive emotions of interest and gratitude are linked to enhanced satisfaction with one's co-workers and supervisors. Positive emotions not only enhance satisfaction with the job, they also reduce turnover intentions and reduce effects of stress and work pressure on employees.

List of words used to reflect Positive emotion

- **Joy-** A sense of elation, happiness, and perhaps even exhilaration, often experienced as a sudden spike due to something good happening.
- **Gratitude-** A feeling of thankfulness, for something specific or simply all encompassing, often accompanied by humility and even reverence.
- **Serenity-** A calm and peaceful feeling of acceptance of oneself.
- **Interest-** A feeling of curiosity or fascination that demands and captures your attention.

- **Hope** – A feeling of optimism and anticipation about a positive future.
- **Pride-** A sense of approval of oneself and pleasure in an achievement, skill, or personal attribute.
- **Amusement-** A feeling of light hearted pleasure and enjoyment, often accompanied by smiles and easy laughter.
- **Inspiration-** Feeling engaged, uplifted and motivated by something.
- **Awe-** An emotion that is evoked when you witness something ground, spectacular, or sparking a sense of overwhelming appreciation.
- **Elevation-** The feeling you get when you see someone engaging in an act of kindness, generosity, or inner goodness, spurring you to aspire to similar actions.
- **Altruism-** Usually referred to as an act of selflessness and generosity towards others, but can also be described as the feeling you get from helping others.
- **Satisfaction-** A sense of pleasure and contentment felt by accomplishing something or fulfilling a need.
- **Relief-** The feeling of happiness one experiences when an uncertain situation turns out for the best, or a negative outcome does not happen.
- **Affection-** An emotional attachment to someone or something accompanied by a liking for them and a sense of pleasure in their company.
- **Cheerfulness-** A feeling of brightness.
- **Surprise-** A sense of delight when someone brings you unexpected happiness or a situation goes even better than you had hoped.
- **Confidence-** Emotion involving a strong sense of self-esteem and belief in yourself; can be specific to a situation or activity, or more universal.

- **Admiration-** A feeling of warm approval, respect, and appreciation for someone or something.
- **Enthusiasm-** A sense of excitement, accompanied by motivation and engagement.
- **Eagerness-** It is like a less intense form of enthusiasm, a feeling of readiness and excitement for something.
- **Euphoria-** Intense and the all-inclusive sense of joy, happiness, often experienced when something extremely positive and exciting happens.
- **Contentment** – Peaceful, comforting, and low-key sense of happiness and well-being.
- **Enjoyment-** A feeling of taking pleasure in what is going on around you; especially in situations like a leisure activity or social gathering.
- **Optimism-** Positive and hopeful emotions that encourage you to look forward to a bright future; one in which you believe that things will mostly work out.
- **Happiness-** A feeling of pleasure and contentment; a general sense of enjoyment and enthusiasm for life.
- **Love-** The strongest of all positive emotions, love is a feeling of deep and continuing affection for someone, along with a willingness to put other's needs ahead of one's own. It can be directed towards an individual, a group of people, or even all humanity.

Our emotions are the driving powers of our lives. We cannot see the wind; but we only see its effects on trees. In the same way, though emotion itself is invisible; we only see its effects on the face and body.

In general, positive emotions include feelings such as appreciation, joy, love, passion, excitement, and freedom. Research suggests that the very act of reflecting on some of the good things that happen to us actually contributes to our well-being. We should focus on the positive feelings rather than lamenting over the negative experiences in our life.

Even on a bad day, some good things may happen in disguise. It is important that we must perceive the positivity, accept it, and move on with a positive mind. Most people like to feel good and positive emotions generate 'feel good' effects. Sometimes there may not be any specific reasons to feel good; we just do. Experiencing emotions like happiness, excitement, joy, hope, and inspiration is vital for anyone who wants to lead a happy life.

Positive Traits and Positive Subjective Experiences

Positive Psychology is the scientific study of positive individual traits and positive experiences. It is a field concerned with well-being and optimal functioning and aims at broadening the focus of psychology beyond sufferings. Positive psychology indicates that people aspire for satisfaction, contentment, and joy in life instead of sadness and worry. Moreover, people who suffer want to build their strengths and not just correct their weaknesses (Duckworth, Steen and Seligman, 2005). Positive psychology focuses on the positive events and effects in life, including:

- Positive states and traits (gratitude, resilience, and compassion).
- Positive experiences (happiness, joy, inspiration, and love).
- Positive institutions (applying positive principles within the entire organizations and institutions).

Traits are enduring personal characteristics that influence behaviour, cognition and affect (Matthews et al., 2009). Understanding positive individual traits consists of the study of strengths and virtues, such as the capacity for love and work, courage and compassion, resilience, creativity, curiosity, integrity, self-knowledge, moderation, self-control, and wisdom. Psychology focused most of its attention on human sufferings. Marked progress has been made in understanding and treating numerous psychological disorders i.e. depression, anxiety, and phobias, to name a few. While trying to reduce sufferings, however, psychology has not paid much attention to what makes life most worth living and meaningful. Psychology believes that people want more than just an end to their sufferings. People are keen on leading a meaningful and fulfilling life, and to cultivate what is best within them and at the same time enhancing their experiences of love, work and play. Positive psychology offers a platform that not only heals psychological damage but also builds strengths to enable people to achieve the best things in life. Positive subjective experiences involve the study of contentment with the past, happiness in the present, and hope for the future. Positive institutions entail the study of the strengths that foster better communities, such as justice, responsibility, civility, nurturance, work ethics, leadership, and teamwork. Positive psychology's primary focus is on what people do right to obtain and maintain optimum happiness by striving to understand and help people develop qualities that lead to greater personal fulfilment (Crompton, 2005). The proposition of positive psychology is to promote factors that allow individuals to thrive and flourish by encouraging a change of focus in psychology from a preoccupation with repairing the worst things to a greater emphasis on discovering and building upon positive qualities. Positive psychology aims to identify, study, and enhance those qualities that improve the positive subjective experiences and adaptive personality traits of individuals (Robbins, 2008). It recognizes that people adopt and adjust to life in highly creative ways allowing them to feel good about life. In this context, it has a keen interest in finding out what works and what is right with individuals and the way they choose to live their life, work, and relate to others in their life space. At the individual level, positive psychology is about positive individual traits i.e. the capacity for love, courage, interpersonal skills, aesthetic sensibility, perseverance, forgiveness, originality, spirituality, high talent, and wisdom. At the group level, it is about virtues and institutions that move individuals towards better citizenship, responsibility, nurturance, altruism, civility, moderation, tolerance and work ethics.

Major Positive Traits

Creativity- Creativity is a phenomenon whereby something new and somehow valuable is formed. The created item may be intangible i.e. an idea, a scientific theory, a musical composition) or a physical object i.e. an invention, a printed literary work, or a painting. Creativity, in general, is usually different from innovation. Innovation is the creation, development and implementation of a new product, process or service, with the aim of improving efficiency, effectiveness or competitive change. In the **Wallas Stage Model (1926)**, Wallas presented one of the first models of the creative process. The creative insights and illuminations have been explained by a process consisting of five stages:

- **Preparation:** Preparatory work on a problem that focuses the individual's mind on the problem and explores the problem's dimensions.
- **Incubation:** The problem is internalized into the unconscious and nothing appears externally to be happening.
- **Intimation:** The creative person gets a 'feeling' that a solution is on its way.
- **Illumination or insight:** The creative idea bursts forth from its preconscious processing into conscious awareness.
- **Verification:** The idea is consciously verified, elaborated and then applied.

Wallas model is often treated as four stages, with 'intimation' seen as a sub-stage. Guilford drew a distinction between convergent and divergent thinking in explaining creativity. **Convergent thinking** involves aiming for a single correct answer to standard questions. **Divergent thinking** is a thought process or method used to generate creative ideas by exploring many possible solutions. Divergent thinking is sometimes used as a synonym for creativity. Guilford (1950) hypothesized one of the first models for the components of creativity. He explained that creativity is expressed through useful problem-solving behaviours and good communicating skills. There are mainly three reasons why people are motivated to be creative:

- Need for novel, varied, and complex stimulation.
- Need to communicate ideas and values.
- Need to solve problems.

In order to be creative, you need to view things in novel ways or from a different perspective. Among other things, you need to be able to generate new possibilities or new alternatives. Tests of creativity measure not only the number of alternatives that people can generate but the uniqueness of those alternatives. The ability to generate alternatives or to see things uniquely does not occur by chance; it is linked to often more fundamental qualities of thinking, such as flexibility, tolerance of ambiguity or unpredictability and the enjoyment of unexplored areas. Creativity is inventing, experimenting, growing, taking risks, breaking rules, making mistakes, and facing funs. It involves breaking out of expected patterns in order to look at things in a different way. In the process the person may commit mistakes; however, he, who never makes a mistake, never tries out new things. Hence, one cannot exhaust creativity. The more one uses creativity, the more he/she has. If we want to live in a creative way, we should not look back too much. One has to invest time in oneself to have great experiences that are going to enrich. Creativity comes from a conflict of ideas which is a natural extension of our enthusiasm. Energy is the key to creativity. It is the ability to introduce order into the randomness of nature. A creative life is an amplified life; to be creative means to be in love with life. Every day is an opportunity to be creative. Creativity is the ability to generate new ideas or concepts, or new associations between ideas and known concepts, which usually produce original solutions. By believing passionately in something that still does not exist, we create it. An idea that is developed and put into action is more important than an idea that exists only as an idea. Creativity does not need to be a herculean event. But it does need consistent fostering. The canvas is the mind, the contents are the thoughts and feelings, the panorama is the story and the complete picture becomes an art. We should be careful of what we put on the canvas of our mind, as it affects our life in the long run. Creativity is the quality that is reflected in your activity. It is an attitude, an inner approach; how you look at things. Whatsoever you do, if you do it with love, then it is creative. Great things are not done by impulse, but through a series of small things brought together. The desire to create is one of the deepest desires of human being. Creativity is not the finding of a thing, but it is the process of making something new out of it. It is simply deviation from the established patterns to look at things in a different way. The important point is one has to be alert, question, and find out so that one's own initiative may be awakened. Since the creative person is willing to live with ambiguity and intensely believes in something that still does not exist, he is able to create a new thing out of that ambiguity.

Characteristics of the Creative Personality

- Most creative persons are very **passionate and intense** about their work, yet they can be extremely objective about it as well. They alternate between fantasy and reality.
- The more liberal a person is, the more creative he can be since creativity is the greatest expression of **liberty**.
- Creative persons develop a **romantic relationship with life**. It is only when people are in love with their lives they cultivate capacity for infinite creativity.
- Creative individuals are **energetic and adventurous**.
- Creative individuals tend to be smart, yet they are often found to be introverts. Hence, there is **unpredictability** in their behaviour.
- Creative people are **visionary**; they have the ability to visualize in their imagination.

- Creative people are curious of everything since **curiosity** is an asset of creativity.
- Creative people are **fearless.** They are brave enough to commit mistakes and do not get panicky for being punished.
- Sometimes creative people are perceived to be **slightly abnormal** in their approach to life since the most talented, thought- provoking, game-changing people often deviate from the standard norms of the society.
- An artist paints; a poet writes; a dancer depicts different dance forms though his/ her body postures and expressions. Creative people **encroach into the unknown** rather than the known territory. This makes them creative and unique.
- Creative people **express themselves in full**. To live is to express, and to express you have to create. Creation is not mere repetition; rather it is to do a common thing in an uncommon way.

Curiosity: Curiosity or inquisitiveness is life. Anyone who keeps learning irrespective of age stays young. We try to teach our children by using 'fear' at the background. This **fear** factor should be replaced by **curiosity** and **interest** to make learning process easier and more effective. Curiosity is the fuel for discovery, inquiry, and learning. Curiosity when coupled with **fearlessness** and **determination** becomes one of the most valuable characteristics one can possess. The important point is not to stop questioning when we listen with curiosity, we should not listen with the intent to reply; we must listen for what is behind the words.

Courage: One is not necessarily born with courage, but one is born with potential. Without courage, we cannot practice any other virtue with consistency. We cannot become kind, true, merciful, generous, or honest without courage. It is not the strength of the body that counts, but the **strength of the spirit** which is the real courage of the individual. Courage is not only the absence of fear, but the victory over it. The brave man is not only fearless, but he also conquers that fear. It is the simple, quiet, unreserved strength to keep moving despite the fear we have. When you are not ready to take risk, you cannot grow. If you cannot grow, you cannot be successful in your life. A ship is safe in harbour, but that is not what ship is meant for. Courage is the most important of all the virtues. You can choose courage, or you can choose comfort, but you cannot choose both. It is risking the known for the unknown, the familiar for unfamiliar. We should face our destiny with courage. Courage is a decision; it is the little voice at the end of the day that says, "I will try again tomorrow". Byrne et al., (2000) identified the three types of courage as physical, moral, and vital courage. **Physical courage** involves the maintenance of societal good by the expression of physical behaviour grounded in the pursuit of socially valued goals. **Moral courage** is the behavioural expression of authenticity in the face of discomfort, disapproval, or rejection. **Vital courage** refers to the perseverance through a disease or disability even when the outcome is ambiguous. It is the inspiration for actions that ultimately promote survival.

Compassion: Compassion for others begins with kindness to ourselves. One of the secrets of inner peace is the practice of compassion. However, it is not enough to be compassionate; one must act accordingly. Since compassion is an action word with no boundaries, it is to look beyond your own pain to see the pain of others. It is the threads that connects human to each other. Compassion is the **keen awareness of the interdependence** of all things. It is passion with a heart. Humanity survives and flourishes when we use our voice for kindness, ears for compassion, hands for charity, mind for truth, and heart for love. When you have real compassion for others, you can recognize love. We must know that there is nobility in compassion, beauty in empathy, and grace in forgiveness. Compassion is a feeling of deep sympathy for another who is suffering due to lack or loss and it is accompanied by a strong desire to alleviate the sufferings. It is the desire that extends the individual self to enlarge the scope of its self-concern to embrace the whole of the universal self.

Self-Control: Self-control is a trait, which describes the **self-regulation** of an individual and indicates the individual's disciplined use of will power. By this self-imposed constraint, one can be able to control the negative aspects of emotion like anger, jealousy, and aggressiveness. A self-controlled person is calm, patient, inhibited, and conscientious. Self-control is essential to success. People are able to control themselves in order to do what needs to be done to make them successful. Some people lack self-control over themselves, which makes them a loser. Self-control is strength and one's greatest challenge is to control oneself. We must know that it is not necessary to react to everything you notice since silence is not always a sign of weakness; it is also a sign of strong self-control. Self-control is all about moment to moment **self-awareness**. Mentally strong people keep control on their mind and are prepared to work and succeed on their own merits. They spend their mental energy and think productively. Most of our stress comes from the way we respond to the situations. A moment of patience in a moment of anger saves a hundred moments of regret. By constant **self-discipline and self-control** we can develop strength and power of mind. Hence, the ultimate expression of power is self-control. Self-disciplined behaviour protects our health and well-being.

Integrity: By integrity and genuineness, it is meant more than just telling the truth to others. We represent us to others and to ourselves in the most sincere way. Integrity is making sure that the things we say and the things we do are in alignment. It is doing the right thing, even when no one is watching. Integrity lies in doing what one speaks; speaking what one does. It is not a destination. It is a way of life. It is an **internal guidance system** that will never guide you astray. When you are able to maintain your own highest standards of integrity regardless of what others may do; you are destined for greatness. We all know that the qualities of great men are vision, integrity, courage, understanding, and the power of articulation. Integrity is the foundation for achievement. It takes courage to create a meaningful life of integrity. It also requires good company and practice. The level of integrity, ethical behaviour, and sense of fairness contribute to our mental health. Integrity of people is to be assessed by their conduct, not by their hierarchical position in their profession. Creating a culture of **integrity and accountability** not only improves the **quality of life** but also facilitates our **well-being**. The greatness of a man is determined by his integrity and his ability to affect those around him positively. We should have the courage to say 'No' and the courage to face the truth. We must do right thing because it is 'right'. We should support the truth, even when it is not acceptable. These are the magic keys to life with integrity. One should never compromise with one's integrity.

Positive subjective Experiences indicate the degree to which people are achieving a goal based on what they believe to be important. A subjective experience refers to the emotional and cognitive impact of human experience as opposed to an objective experience which is the actual events of the experience. While something objective is tangible and can be experienced by others, subjective experiences are produced by the **individual mind.** While quite real to the person experiencing a subjective experience are often profound, it cannot be objectively or empirically measured by others. For thousands of years, human beings are fascinated by **beauty, truth, love, honour, altruism, courage, social relationships,** etc. All these taken together or in separate entity constitute positive subjective experiences. The joy of life becomes really enjoyable when we gather new experiences. Person, place, or anything of our interest brings happiness and positive spirit into our life. We must look for ways which will be an active force in our lives. When we smile it radiates a positive energy that makes people feel comfortable around us. Once we replace negative thoughts with positive ones, we will start having positive results. People with a vision of the possibilities to attain new levels of experience are benefited from the courage to live their dreams. We never like to remain stagnant; all of us need to grow continuously in our lives. We are never too old to set another goal or to dream a new dream. In the context of positive subjective experiences the following factors may be discussed in detail.

Pleasure: Pleasure is **multi-dimensional**. Although we often focus on pleasure to be derived from an object; we do also experience pleasure from reminiscing past memories and visualizing future outcomes. When we think about past pleasures, our memories are influenced by the intensity of the immediate experience as well as how it ended, a formula termed as **peak-end-theory** by Kahneman (1999). The peak-end-rule is **psychological heuristic** in which people judge an experience largely based on how they felt at its peak and at its end, rather than based on the total sum or average of every moment of the experience. The effect occurs regardless of whether the experience is pleasant or unpleasant. It is concluded that people remember experiences essentially based on how they feel at its peak and at its end, rather than their experience overall. Kahneman attributes this cognitive tendency to evolutionary purposes. He states, "Memory was not designed to measure ongoing happiness, or total sufferings". Kahneman describes two types of 'selves', the **experiencing self** and the **narrating self**. The experiencing self is our **moment to moment awareness** and **being present**. This mode of thinking is intuitive, quick, and unconscious. The experiencing self does not remember events, and each moment of the experiencing self lasts three seconds. The narrating self is what collects and integrates our experiences and creates narratives that we experience as our memory. Our **narrating self does a lot of editing and interpretation**. During this process, changes in our stories occur. Thus, the **peak-end-effect** is a **cognitive shortcut** our brain uses by focusing our memories on the most intense aspects of an experience and what the ending is like. Peterson & Kozhokar (2017) explored the perceptions of workload ratings. Results confirmed that subjective workload ratings are also impacted by the peak-end-effects. Research supports that an event with a pleasurable peak at the end will be remembered positively. Studies have shown that adding a positive end to a pleasant exercise session will impact the decision to repeat the exercise. It is suggested that a peak moment requires at least one of the four elements below, with the best having all four:

- **Elevation:** These are moments of **happiness** that transcend the normal course of events through sensory pleasures and surprise.
- **Pride**: These are moments that capture us at our best; whether it is **moments of achievement** or **moments of courage**.
- **Insight**: These are our **Eureka moments**: the capacity to gain deep understanding and give a moment of sobering clarity.
- **Connection**: These are moments which are social in nature like birthday party, wedding ceremony or any other group celebration. It is turned out that how long an experience lasts or continues is not very important. Kahneman and Fredrickson named this as; **duration neglect**. It is the psychological recognition that people's judgements of the unpleasantness experiences depend very little on the duration of those experiences of (Kahneman& Fredrickson, 1993). Cognitive biases change the way that we recall past events. The peak-end-rule focuses our memories around the most intense moments of an experience and the way an experience ends. In Kahneman's words, we remember experiences in our lives as a series of snapshots rather than a complete catalogue of events. Our minds quickly average the moments that most stand out in our memories to form our opinion of the past. The most emotionally intense points of an experience and the end of that experience are heavily weighted in how we remember an event. The last expressions are lasting impressions. When we remember an episode in the past, the most recent events are activated quickly in our memories. In reviewing the research literature on the prediction of pleasure, Loewenstein and Schkade (1999) pointed out the following effects:

Mere Exposure Effect: The mere exposure effect refers to our tendency to like objects to which we are frequently exposed, even if this exposure takes place subliminally. It is a psychological phenomenon by which people tend to develop a preference for things merely because they are familiar with them. In social psychology, this effect is sometimes called the **familiarity principle.** It is only required that the stimulus is merely shown, however, briefly or incidentally, to the individual. Mere exposure to an object can lead to more liking, and thus a more positive attitude toward the object. The mere-exposure effect posits that repeated exposure to a stimulus increases **perceptual fluency**, the ease with which a stimulus can be processed. Perceptual fluency, in turn, increases positive affect. It makes natural that familiarity breeds liking. Hence, things that are familiar are likely to be safer and acceptable than unknown and unfamiliar things.

Endowment Effect: Such effect suggests that people are pleased with **what they have** and **what is familiar**. It is an emotional bias that causes individuals to value an owned object higher, often irrationally than its objective value (Kahneman et al., 1991). This bias occurs when we overvalue something that we own. People are pleased with what they have and with what are familiar to them.

Adaptation: Adaptation is a familiar experience for all of us. A psychological adaptation is a functional, cognitive or behavioural trait that falls under the scope of **evolved psychological mechanisms**. Adaptation refers to an individual's ability to adjust to changes and new experiences, and to accept new information. The ability to adapt helps us to grow mentally. Adaptation to pleasure is so common and natural that it is said that we live on a hedonic treadmill. We adapt to improving circumstances to the point that we always return to a point of relative neutrality (Brickman & Campbell, 1971). The hedonic treadmill, also known as hedonic adaptation is the observed tendency of human to quickly return to a relatively stable level of happiness despite major positive or negative events or life changes.

People achieve greater life satisfaction when they work for things they value, rather than working merely for immediate pleasure. Hence, people having clear goals make progress and report high level of positive subjective experiences. Moreover, psychological measures such as self-esteem ensure more positive subjective experiences in individualistic societies compared to collective societies. We should gather knowledge about our strengths and talents to maximize our achievements which would lead to more of positive subjective experiences.

Flow and Happiness

Flow: A very well-known topic in positive psychology is **flow.** The concept of flow was first scientifically explored and defined by Csikszentmihalyi (1990). Csikszentmihalyi research led him to conclude that **happiness** is an internal state of being, not an external one. His popular book, **"Flow: The psychology of optimal Experience"** is based on the belief that happiness levels can be shifted by introducing flow. **Flow** is defined as an optimal state of engagement, happiness and peak experience that occurs when an individual is absorbed in an intrinsically motivating challenge. The state of flow has been implicated in the pathways to happiness and thus expands further the concept of happiness beyond the pleasure state. Through research, it is understood that people are more creative, productive, and happy when they are in a state of flow. Athletes, musicians, and artists described their optimal states of performance as instances when their work simply flowed out of them without much effort. The **metaphor of flow** is one that many people have used to describe the sense of effortless action; they feel in moments that stand out as the best in their lives. It is sometimes called **being in the zone, ecstasy,** or **aesthetic rapture.** Csikszentmihalyi describes the conditions where it tends to occur i.e. there are goals that require appropriate responses; there is immediate feedback; there is a challenge where one's skills match the level of skill required. A person in flow is completely focused, without distracting thoughts. One's sense of time is distorted. The activity is done for its own sake. It is explained that, it is the full involvement of flow, rather than happiness that makes excellence in life. Flow is a state in which people are so involved in an activity that nothing else seems to matter, the experience is so enjoyable that people continue to do it even at great cost, for the pure sake of doing it. It is found that the most satisfying and productive work involves a level of challenge appropriate to our skill that actively engages our talents and produces a sense of **vital engagement** and **flow.** In flow, we are out of our minds in the sense of breaking through the dominance of normal consciousness (Csikszentmihalyi, 2002). The best moments usually occur when a person's body and mind are stretched to their limits in a voluntary effort to accomplish something difficult and worthwhile. The experience of flow is universal and has been reported to occur across all classes, genders, ages, and cultures. It can be experienced during many types of activities. It was observed by Csikszentmihalyi that many people were not able to live life of contentment when their jobs, homes, and security were lost during World War II. After the war, Csikszentmihalyi took an interest in art, philosophy, and religion as a means to answer the question, "what creates a life worth living"? He realized that to overcome the anxieties and depressions of contemporary life, individuals must become independent of the social environment to the degree that they no longer respond exclusively in terms of its rewards and punishments. One has to learn to provide rewards to oneself to achieve such autonomy. The person has to develop the ability to find enjoyment and purpose regardless of external circumstances. Again, most enjoyable activities are not natural; they demand efforts that initially one is reluctant to make. However, once the person is being allowed to get feedback of his performance, it becomes intrinsically rewarding. It is when we act freely; for the sake of the actions itself rather than for any other ulterior motives, we begin to enjoy the process of learning. People who learn to control inner experiences determine the quality of their lives, and feel happy naturally. Happiness is not a rigid, unchanging state. Beyond each person's set point of happiness, there is a level of happiness over which each individual has some degree of control. Through research, it is found that people are their most creative, productive, and happy selves, when they are in a state of flow.

Components of flow: In positive psychology, a flow state, also known as **being in the zone**, is the mental state in which a person performing an activity is fully immersed in a feeling of energized focus, full involvement and enjoyment in the process of the activity. In essence, flow is characterized by the complete absorption in what one does, and a resulting transformation in one's sense of time. According to Csikszentmihalyi, there are nine major components of flow.

Balance between skills and challenge: Flow requires an equal balance between the skill level and the challenge. When it is too simple, we get bored. In a flow experience, we feel engaged by the challenge, and at the same time we are not overstressed by the difficulty level of the task.

Merging of Action and Awareness: We may often get confused and disturbed over thinking 'what could have been done', 'what might have been done', and 'what should be done' while doing the task at hand. However, in 'flow' we are completely **absorbed in the task** at hand since we do not leave any space to think otherwise.

Clear Goals: In many of our everyday situations, there are demands which are contradictory to each other. It put us in a dilemma. However, in a flow experience, we have a clear picture and good grasp of our assignment and accountability.

Immediate feedback: In flow, direct and indirect feedbacks are continuously available, so that we are able to constantly adjust our reactions to meet the current demands. When we are in flow, we know about our **progress**.

Concentration on the task at hand: High level of concentration excludes unnecessary distractions. Since we are absorbed in the activity, we are only aware of what is relevant to the task at hand, and do not think about other unrelated things. Being **totally connected to the task** at hand epitomizes the flow state and it is one of its most unique characteristics. The performer gives his hundred percent attention to the task.

Sense of control: An absolute sense of personal control exists over the situation or activity, as if we are able to do anything we aspire for.

Loss of Self-Consciousness: A lack of awareness of bodily needs as self-consciousness disappears. We often are too conscious about others' opinion on ourselves. In a flow state, we get so involved in our own activity that we ignore others' feedback.

Transformation of time: In flow state, a distorted sense of time occurs. Time either slows down or flies by when we are completely engaged in the moment. These sensations come about through the intense involvement of a flow experience.

Autotelic Experience: Flow is an intrinsically rewarding activity; the activity becomes **autotelic,** an end in itself, done for its own sake. Flow is a state of absorption in one's work characterized by the intense concentration, loss of self-awareness, a feeling of being perfectly challenged (neither bored nor overwhelmed), and a sense that **time is flying**. Anyone can experience flow in many different regards, such as play, creativity, and work. To experience flow, one needs to have the correct ratio of challenge for their particular skill set. Autotelic experience is a final result of the above described dimensions of flow, and it is an essential motivational component which propels an individual to greater and greater challenges.

Conditions of flow: A flow state can be entered while performing any activity, although it is most likely to occur when one is wholeheartedly performing a task or activity for intrinsic purposes. While the activities that induce flow may vary and be multifaceted, Csikszentmihalyi asserts that the experience of flow is similar despite the nature of the activity. It is to be mentioned that the components of flow can appear independently of each other, but only in combination they constitute 'flow' experience. Flow theory postulates three conditions that have to be satisfied to achieve a flow state:

- One must be involved in an activity with a **clear set of goals and progress**. This adds direction and structure to the task.
- The task at hand must have clear and immediate feedback. This helps the person negotiate any changing demands and allows them to adjust their performance to maintain the flow state.
- There should be a **good balance** between the perceived challenge of the task at hand and the perceived skills. One must have confidence in one's ability to complete the task at hand. However, it is argued that the antecedent factors of flow are interrelated, i.e. a perceived balance between challenges and skills, clear goals, and knowledge about the progress in achieving the goal (immediate feedback).

Who experiences flow? The capacity to experience flow may differ from person to person. Csikszentmihalyi hypothesized that people with very specific personality traits are more likely to achieve and enjoy flow more often than the average person. These personality traits include **curiosity, persistence, low self-centeredness,** and a **high rate of performing activities** for intrinsic reasons only. People with most of these personality traits are said to have an **autotelic personality**. Studies suggest that those with autotelic personalities tend to experience more flow. The term **autotelic** is acquired from two Greek words, 'auto' meaning self, and 'telos' meaning goal. Being autotelic means having a **self-contained activity**, one that is done without any expectation of some future benefits, but simply 'experiencing the activity itself' as the main goal. It is found that people with an autotelic personality have a greater preference for **high-action-opportunity** and **high-skills situations** that stimulate them and encourage growth. It is in such high-challenge, high-skills situations that people are most likely to enter the flow state. It is suggested that enhancing the time spent on flow makes our lives more happy and successful. Flow experiences lead to positive affect and better performance. Furthermore, to overcome the anxieties and depressions of contemporary life, on some occasions, people should make themselves independent of impressions of the social environment. Hence, they no longer are constrained by rewards and punishments at the cost of sacrificing their hobbies and interests. Within flow, we have a sense of control, even when engaged in very risky activities. It is observed that, **what people enjoy is not the sense of being in control, but the sense of exercising control in difficult situations.** Researchers find a positive correlation between flow and conscientiousness and negative correlation between flow and neuroticism (Ullen et al., 2012). It can be said that neurotic individuals are more prone to anxiety and self-criticism, which disrupt a flow state. On the contrary, conscientious individuals are more likely to spend time mastering challenging tasks thoroughly. Indeed, flow can be described as a key aspect of **eudaimonia, or self-actualization** in an individual. Since it is intrinsically rewarding, the more you practice it, the more you seek to repeat these experiences which leads to a fully engaged and happy life.

Mechanisms of flow: The key contribution of positive psychology towards understanding of the qualities and attributes of well-being is the concept of flow. Flow is an optimal state of engagement, happiness, and peak experience that occurs when an individual is absorbed in an intrinsically motivating challenge. In a given moment, there is a great deal of information made available to each individual. Psychologists have found that mind can attend to only a certain amount of information at a time. For the most part, people are able to decide what they want to focus their attention on. However, when one is in the flow state, they are completely engrossed with the task at hand and without making the conscious decision to do so, lose awareness of all other things: time, people, distractions, and even basic bodily needs. According to Csikszentmihalyi, this occurs because all the attention of the person in the flow state is concentrated on the task and there is no more surplus attention to be distributed otherwise. The flow state has been described as the **optimal experience** in that one gets a level of high gratification from the experience. This flow experience is idiosyncratic and depends on the concerned individual. Flow is typically characterized by being immersed in a specific activity that incorporates the following mechanisms:-

- **Concentration** towards the task at hand appears effortless and is not associated with mental stress and strain to repress or control thinking.
- **Involvement** in the task to the point where there is no need to think about what needs to be done before it is taken care of.
- **Enjoyment** through being involved in and doing the specific activity at hand.

Positive consequences of flow: Flow is an innately positive experience; it is known to produce intense feelings of enjoyment. It is an experience that is so enjoyable that it creates positive affect and happiness in the long run. **Happiness** is derived from personal development and growth and flow nurtures the experience of personal development. When the person under the experience of flow is fully focused and directed to one thing, it leads to **improved performance**. Researchers found that flow can enhance performance in a wide variety of areas including teaching, learning, athletics, and artistic creativity. Flow encourages one to absorb information, synthesize, and integrate it. This propels the **creative process**. People in flow use this state to take performance to the next level. Flow leads to further **learning and skill development**. Since the act of achieving flow indicates a substantial mastery of a certain skill, the individual must continuously seek new scope and challenges in order to maintain this state. In positive psychology, a flow state, also known as **being in the zone**, is the mental state in which a person performing an activity is fully immersed in a feeling of energized focus, full involvement, and enjoyment in the process of the activity. In essence, flow is characterized by the complete absorption in what one does, and a resulting transformation in one's sense of time. Whatever produces flow becomes its own reward. Since there is no awareness of the self during a flow state, physical and mental functions become one. Moreover, individuals experience not only satisfaction and catharsis; they often also exceed their usual levels of performance (Jackson, 1992). As such flow has been associated with **peak levels of experience and peak levels of performance** (Privette, 1981).

Negative Consequences of flow: In the above paragraphs flow has been described as an optimal state which results in peak performance. However, the consequences of experiencing flow may not always be beneficial. We all know that flow is a state of optimal experience, a state in which people are so involved in an activity that nothing else seems to matter. The experience itself is so enjoyable that people do it even at great cost, for the pure sake of doing it (Cskszentmihalyi, 1991). Flow has been depicted as the ultimate **autotelic experience**; one that is performed purely for its own ends. Part of the pleasure of flow comes from its **dissociative nature,** via the transcendence of the self that takes place (Stranger, 1999).

Cskszentmihalyi (2002) suggested that flow can have **addictive properties**, explaining that the self becomes captive of a certain kind of order, and is then unwilling to cope with other priorities of life. The individual may be driven perpetually to recreate flow. There is a need to consider that while flow may be associated with peak performance, it may also be associated with other less positive outcomes. This is not intended to say that flow itself is either good or bad; rather that such a state may be associated with both positive and negative consequences.

Meaning and Nature of Happiness

The concept of happiness is the cornerstone of the assumption of positive psychology. **Happiness** is that feeling when we know that **life is good**. In other words, happiness is a **sense of well-being, joy**, and **contentment.** The term 'happiness' is used in the context of mental or emotional states including positive or pleasant emotions which range from contentment to intense joy. Happiness in its broad sense is the label for a conglomeration of **pleasant emotional states**. It is also used in the context of **life satisfaction, flourishing, and well-being**. In understanding happiness, there are two main theoretical perspectives which focus on addressing the question of what makes people feel good and happy. The two approaches to happiness i.e. hedonic and eudaimonic approaches are often quoted to explain happiness. **Hedonic approach** is based on the notion that increased pleasure and decreased pain leads to happiness which is in line with subjective well-being. **Subjective well-being** is a term that is commonly used to denote the **happy or good life**. It comprises of an affective component i.e. high positive affect and low negative affect and a cognitive component (satisfaction with life). It is to be noted that an individual experiences happiness when positive affect and satisfaction with life are both high. **Eudaimonic well-being,** on the other hand, is strongly associated with Maslow's idea of self-actualization and Roger's concept of the fully functioning person. **Eudaimonic happiness** is, therefore, based on the concept that people feel happy when they have a **sense of control of autonomy, feeling of meaning and purpose, sense of belongingness, social contribution, competence, and personal growth.** This approach adopts self-determination theory to conceptualize happiness. **Self-determination theory** suggests that happiness is related to fulfilment in the areas of autonomy and competence. From this perspective by engaging in eudaimonic pursuits, subjective well-being (happiness) occurs as a by-product. Thus, life purpose and higher order meaning are believed to produce happiness. It implies that happiness does not result from the pursuit of pleasure only but from the development of individual strengths and virtues. Moreover, the pursuit of happiness is real. We all want to be happy. Happiness is a direction; not a destination. The true secret of happiness lies in taking a genuine interest in all the details of daily life. Happiness is not something ready-made. It comes from our thoughts and actions. It is the spiritual experience of living every minute with love, grace, and gratitude. People should find happiness in little things. It is largely a choice; not a right or entitlement. Happiness is the meaning and the purpose of life, the aim and end of human existence.

Sources of happiness: Positive psychology emphasizes how to cultivate the power of maximizing the potential for happiness in many of our everyday behaviours. Each of these findings gives us a concrete idea for improving our quality of life. The happiness of our life depends upon the nature of our thoughts. Our life is an expression of all our thoughts. We tend to forget that happiness does not come as a result of getting something we do not have, but rather from recognizing and appreciating what we do have. We must know that the search for happiness is one of the chief sources of unhappiness. Three grand essentials to happiness in life are 'something to do', 'something to love', and 'something to hope for'. Happiness is a form of courage. The person who can bring the spirit of laughter into a room is indeed blessed. Human beings are always fascinated by beauty, truth, love, honour, altruism, courage, and social relationships that all come under the banner of happiness. It is true that feeling happy and experiencing positive emotions increases the chances of more favourable outcomes to become happy. It is true that the sources of happiness and the reasons to be happy may vary from person to person. However, there are some underlying general factors that contribute to happiness that are given below:

Happiness is infectious: Those with happy friends and significant others are more likely to be happy.

Acts of kindness: People who are kind towards others not only get uplifted, they are also more accepted by their relatives and friend circles which add to their happiness.

Elevation of well-being: Time and effort spent on a cause you believe in, elevates your well-being and life satisfaction and reduces symptoms of depression.

Sharing with others: Seek out others to share the experiences and convey them how much you value the moment. This is a powerful predictor of happiness.

Memory building: Mental photographs or even a physical souvenir of the event, when reminisced, brings lot of happiness.

Self-congratulation: Congratulate yourself 'how great you are' and how long you have waited for this to happen.

Sharpening perception: Focus on certain interesting and relevant elements and block out the rest, like closing your eyes and listening to music.

Absorption: Allow yourself to become totally immersed and try not to get distracted by any other environmental stimuli.

Mindfulness: Sometimes we communicate and react without much thinking. We can focus our perspective and sharpen our experience of the present moment through mindfulness. Mindful attention to the present moment can be developed through meditation.

Avoid forming habits: Repeated indulgence in the same pleasure does not work. It creates monotony. Neurons are wired to respond to novel stimulations, and are not likely to fire when the events do not provide new information. We must seek out a variety of experiences and spread out pleasurable events over time. Surprise yourself or others with small presents of pleasure.

Add meaning to happiness: The satisfaction of one's wants and needs boost happiness, but have virtually no impact on meaningfulness. This indicates that focusing on obtaining what you want increases your happiness. However, you have to add a deeper sense of meaning to make this happiness a permanent feature in your life.

Happiness is present-oriented: Meaningfulness is more focused on the past and future and the way they link to the present. You can focus on the present to increase your happiness.

Givers experience more meaning: When you are in search for meaning, try giving back to others as far as practicable. It is good for our well-being.

Savouring – Amongst the sources of happiness, 'savouring' is an important factor to be discussed in detail. It is the awareness of pleasure and of giving deliberate conscious attention to the experience of pleasure. The basic assumption of savouring is that people have capacities to attend, appreciate, and enhance the positive experiences in their lives. Bryant & Verhoff (2007) believe that whether planned or spontaneous, three preconditions must be satisfied for savouring to occur.

- **First,** person with **focused attention and feelings** may savour a childhood memory or may savour an event which is going to happen in the near future like receiving an award or similar joyful events. Whatever may be the reason, one needs to be fully engrossed for savouring.
- **Second**, to experience savouring, **social and self-esteem needs** must be given **less priority**. When you are too much concerned for the opinion of others or about your ego and self-esteem, you cannot enjoy savouring. Savouring needs an attentive, quiet and relaxed state of mind.
- **Third,** savouring requires a mindful focus on the pleasurable features of a current experience; **fully appreciating one particular thing** rather than thinking of several things that may divert attention away from the present moment and what is in front of us. In savouring, there is no space for analytical thinking. Savouring is a feeling of awe, warmth, comfort, joy, inspiration, happiness, pleasure and contentment. It may begin to occur spontaneously when we are fascinated and begin to appreciate beautiful and pleasurable moments.

Savouring is a relatively simple and straightforward way to enhance our positive experiences. With practice overtime, one may find that savouring becomes a more general mind-set applied to several aspects of life.

Theories of Happiness

Positive psychology attempts to isolate happiness and well-being. Traditionally, happiness has been associated with the moral good (Haidt, 2006). The happiness of an individual is seen as secondary and the only path to it is through morality. The claim of virtue ethics is that morality rests in character. Thus, in acting out virtuous traits, good health, happiness and peace, one must first discipline and control one's own mind. When we can control our mind, we can find the way to enlightenment, and all wisdom and virtue then flow naturally. Even a happy life cannot be free from ups and downs and the word 'happy' would lose its meaning if it were not balanced by 'sadness'. It is wise to accept things as it come with patience and equanimity to move on without worrying too much on happiness. Today's beautiful moments will be tomorrow's beautiful memories. We need not wait for something great to happen to make us happy. We should know how precious the present time is and, therefore, every moment should be enjoyed and savoured in good spirit. Moreover, a happy person is not one in a certain set of circumstances with certain predetermined parameters, but rather a person with a certain set of attitudes. One should surround oneself with people and environments that continually challenge, energize, and literally drive you forward. Being content with simple pleasures increases your opportunity for being happy.

The Set-Point Theory of Happiness

According to this theory of happiness, our level of subjective well-being is determined primarily by **heredity and personality traits** embedded in us early in life. As a result, the happiness level remains constant throughout our lives. The level of happiness may change temporarily in response to life events, however, it returns to its baseline level as we slowly get accustomed to those events and their consequences over time. **Set-point theory of happiness** and well-being assumes that we have an average level of happiness around which our day-to-day and moment-to-moment happiness varies. This is expressed with regard to our temperament, mood and emotion; when our natural temperament is stable with slightly fluctuating moods and emotions.

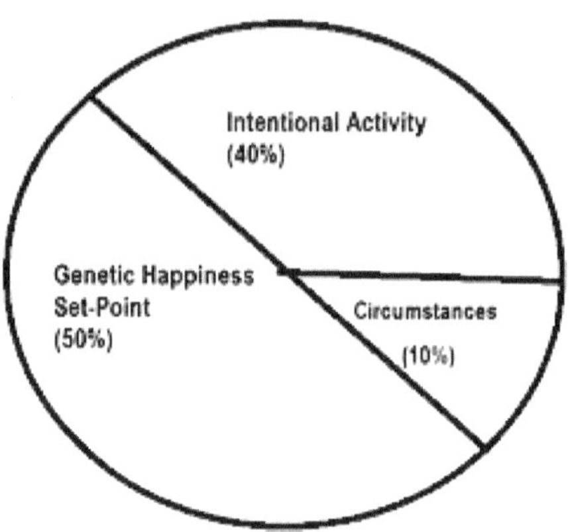

Happiness Set-Point

Source: **Lyubomirsky (2007)**

Genetic studies indicate that there is significant degree of inheritance in many personality factors, as much as fifty percent or so (Lykken & Tellegen, 1996). This implies that the set point may not make up all of a person's happiness but only a part of it. There have also been significant challenges to set-point theory, that life's problems can seriously damage individuals which negatively affects their happiness (Easterlin, 2005). The basic idea of set-point theory is that each individual's general level of happiness is determined by genes. People tend to react differently according to their inherited set point level.

Personality profiles: Personality studies indicate that happy and unhappy people have distinctive personality profiles. Happy people tend to be more **extroverted, optimistic,** and usually have **high self-esteem.** Happiness is also considered to be an emotion produced by positive and negative events and experiences. Research findings show the data that extroverted individuals are happier than introverted individuals in the context of a broad range of life experiences. This has been attributed to the notion that extroverts react more intensely to positive stimuli when compared to introverts. Extroverts are also reported to get along very well with their social environment that may activate positive emotions of happiness. They are sociable and enjoy pleasant interaction with other people that create happiness in and around them. In contrast, unhappy people are believed to be more reactive to unpleasant emotional stimuli compared to their happier counterparts under the same conditions. It is found that **neuroticism** is negatively associated with **subjective well-being (happiness)** while **openness to experience, agreeableness, extraversion,** and **conscientiousness** are positively related to **subjective well-being(happiness)**.

Life Satisfaction and Affective State Theories

The debate over theories of happiness concerns the choice between life satisfaction and affect based views like **hedonism** and the **emotional state theory** (Haybron, 2001). According to emotional state theory of happiness, happiness consists in a broadly positive balance of emotions, moods, and mood propensities. Proponents of **life satisfaction** see two major advantages to their account. Life satisfaction is **holistic**, ranging over the whole of one's life, or the totality of one's life over a certain period of time. It reflects not just the aggregate of moments in one's life, but also the quality of one's life taken as a whole. We are not just concerned about the total quantity of positive happenings in our lives, but about its distribution; a happy ending, say, counts far more than a happy middle (Velleman, 1991). **Life satisfaction theory** identifies happiness with having a favourable attitude toward one's life as a whole. This basic schema can be filled out in a variety of ways, but typically involves some sort of global judgement: an endorsement or affirmation of one's life as a whole. This judgement may be more or less explicit and may also involve or accompany some aggregate of judgements about particular items or domains within one's life. The emotional state view departs from hedonism in a different way i.e. instead of identifying happiness with pleasant experiences it identifies happiness with the **emotional condition** as a whole. This includes non-experiential aspect of emotions and moods, and excludes pleasures that are not directly involved with individual's emotional state.

Research on happiness views that happiness involves three broad categories of affective states:

Endorsement states like joy versus sadness.

Engagement states like flow or a sense of vitality.

Attunement states like tranquillity, emotional expansiveness versus compression, and confidence.

Moreover, happiness does not come from a **state**, but from a **change of state**. Hence, happiness is derived not only from the prize, but in the process of attaining the prize. True happiness is a journey, not a destination. Once that goal is achieved, the satisfaction quickly diminishes until we are left looking for the next high. This condition keeps humanity pushing on to new heights. When we can appreciate each passing moment as a blissful step towards our next destination, there will be lasting happiness. The secret lies in being able to remain content with each passing moment while keeping our eyes on the next. The emotional state theory does not consider the feelings of pleasure but rather the constant emotional background that accompanies us. This is primarily called a state of mind which we would call **serenity** and **contentment** unrelated to specific events or situations. Moreover, in striving for happiness, the most important factor is to have **complete virtue** i.e. good moral character.

Eudaimonia according to Aristotle, **activity expressing virtue** will lead to a happy life. Aristotle (2000) proposed that happiness was neither virtue nor pleasure, but rather the exercise of virtue. **Eudaimonic theory** of happiness argues that rather than the pursuit of pleasure, happiness is the result of the development of individual's strengths and virtues. The theory of eudaimonic happiness has its basis in the concept of the **self-actualizing individual** (Maslow, 1968) and the concept of the **fully functioning person** (Rogers, 1963). Many modern scientific explanations of happiness support the theory of eudaimonic happiness. The eudaimonic theory of happiness adopts the **Self-Determination theory** to conceptualize happiness (Ryan & Deci, 2001). This theory argues that fulfilment in the areas of autonomy and competence enhances happiness. In other words, this view suggests that the subjective well-being i.e. happiness can be achieved through engaging in eudaimonic pursuits.

Happiness is being focused, staying positive and being optimistic. We should always remember how great life is, how it passes us by and how to get pleasure from every moment. Happiness is both a skill and a decision and nothing can make us happy until we choose to be happy.

Altruism, Hope and Optimism

Altruistic emotions and behaviours are associated with **greater well-being, health,** and **longevity.** Theoretically, people who have the benefits of secure social relationships find it easier to understand and respond to other people's sufferings compared with those who have insecure attachments. This is because compassionate reactions are products of what has been called the care giving behavioural system. The optimal functioning of this depends on its not being inhibited by attachment insecurity. **Altruism** is the unselfish concern for other people; doing things simply out of a desire to help. It is not because you feel obliged to do it. Moreover, everyday life is filled with small acts of altruism from holding the door for strangers to helping the needy people.

Altruism act is to promote someone else's welfare even at the risk or cost of ourselves. Evolutionary scientists speculate that altruism has such deep roots in human nature because helping and co-operation promotes the survival of our species. Darwin argued that altruism, which he called **sympathy** or **benevolence** is an essential part of the social instincts. Darwin's claim is supported by recent neuroscience studies, which have shown that when people behave altruistically, their brains activate in regions that signal pleasure and reward. Altruism activates reward centres in the brain. Neurobiologists have found that when engaged in an altruistic act, the pleasure centres of the brain become active. Socialization has an important role in altruistic actions.

Children who observe simple reciprocal acts of altruism are far more likely to exhibit altruistic actions. Thus, it is suggested that modelling altruistic actions can be an important way to foster prosocial and compassionate actions in children. Seligman (2005) commented on a study that linked happiness with altruism. He was under the impression that unhappy people would identify with the sufferings of others and be more altruistic. But to his surprise, it was found that happy people were more likely to demonstrate the altruism trait more than unhappy people. Does it mean altruism helps people to be happy or happiness facilitates altruism? On many levels, psychologically, socially and even physically, one indeed does well by doing good to others (Pillavia, 2003). Kindness in giving creates love. There is abundance of research that backs up the notion that helping others really helps the self (Atkin, Dunn, Whillans, Grant, & Norton, 2013; Knafo & Israel, 2012; Mc Andrew & Perilloux, 2012). Public health researchers have studied the effects of altruistic behaviour on **stress mortality** (Poulin, Brown, Dillard, & Smith, 2013). These researchers found that participating in prosocial acts reduced mortality, while other authors have concluded that helping others leads to deeper relationships and well-being (Post, 2007). Counsellors can use these findings clinically by encouraging their clients to volunteer in organizations that help those in need. In addition, counsellors can explore with their clients how past instances of prosocial behaviour made them feel. Helping others is a true win-win-situation. No person is ever remembered for what he achieves for himself in his life. People are rewarded and recognized only for their contributions to the society.

Altruism and Prosocial Behaviour

Prosocial behaviour covers the broad range of actions intended to benefit one or more people other than oneself; actions such as helping, comforting, sharing, and cooperation. Altruism is motivation to increase another person's welfare. Helping others is associated with higher bench of mental health. When you do good to others, you are actually doing best to yourself. An important ingredient of finding value in oneself is to love others. We can do this in small ways by being kind and helpful, treating others with respect and affirming their dignity as human beings.

Nepotistic Altruism

The first form of altruism is called nepotistic altruism and it is altruism based on family. We all work for our family and make it a mission to provide food, shelter, clothing and all the emotional support our children need to survive and flourish. Parents' hardships and sacrifices for the well-being of their children can be termed as nepotistic altruism.

Reciprocal Altruism

Reciprocal altruism is the second form of altruism, which is altruism seen through a give-and-take relationship. It involves taking actions to help others with an expectation that they offer help in return. Society's rules, norms, and expectations can also influence whether or not people engage in altruistic behaviour. The norm of reciprocity, for example, is a social expectation in which we feel obliged and pressured to help others when the other party has already done some help for us.

Cognitive Reasons and Altruism

While the definition of altruism involves doing good to others without any expectation, there may still be cognitive incentives that are not obvious. For example, we may help others to relieve our own distress or because being kind to others upholds our perception of ourselves as kind, empathetic people. Researchers suggest that people are more likely to engage in altruistic behaviour when they feel empathy for the person who is in distress. This is known as **empathy-altruism hypothesis**.

Negative State relief model: Other researchers stated that altruistic acts help relieve negative feelings created by observing someone else in distress. Essentially, seeing another person in trouble makes us feel upset, distressed, or uncomfortable. By helping the person in trouble helps reduce these negative feelings. Many believe in maximizing wealth and think that by giving, they will lose their bank balance. However, giving is not equivalent to losing. Generosity and kindness are two qualities come from inner bliss which is supreme happiness blended with contentment. It is a simple fact that rivers do not drink their own water and trees do not eat their own fruits. The habit of giving like the river, sun and earth epitomizes the quality of generosity which is the true index of altruism. Kindness in words creates confidence. Kindness in thinking creates profoundness. Kindness in giving creates love. Greatness is not what we have, but it is in what we give. Hence, giving does not mean just giving money and other material things. According to Fromm (1956), the great psychoanalyst, "we should give to others, all that is alive in us i.e. our interest, understanding, knowledge, and humour, everything in us that is good". In doing so, we enhance the sense of aliveness in others while enhancing our own. When we give, we get a **heightened vitality** of what it means to be human.

Further, once giving becomes our attitude, it can be in any form. It can be a kind word, a simple smile or appreciation, sharing knowledge, or giving support to someone during difficult times. 'Giving' in terms of our time, patience, wisdom, compassion, tolerance and caring are worth more than anything money can buy. Altruism is pouring out the goodness of our hearts with no self-serving motives. Too often we underestimate the power of a touch, a smile, a kind word, a listening ear, an honest compliment, or the smallest act of caring, all of which are significant experiences in our lives. When we listen with empathy to another person, we give that person psychological air. Tenderness and kindness which are manifestation of strength and resolution can be our altruistic behaviour. Hence, altruism serves as a catalyst for the warmth and connection that we share with another living being.

Hope and Optimism: Contemporary theories of hope and optimism provide two explanations for how positive expectancies can shape human behaviour and promote well-being. Hope is one of the most powerful forces in humanity, capable of motivating people to move on when they succumb to give up or quit. At times hope is all we have and that is enough. Hopeful thoughts reflect the belief that one can find pathways to desired goals and get inspired to use those pathways. Snyder (1994) studied two visions of optimism; expectancy and agency which are integrated into hope. **Hope is the belief** that our expectations and goals can be achieved.

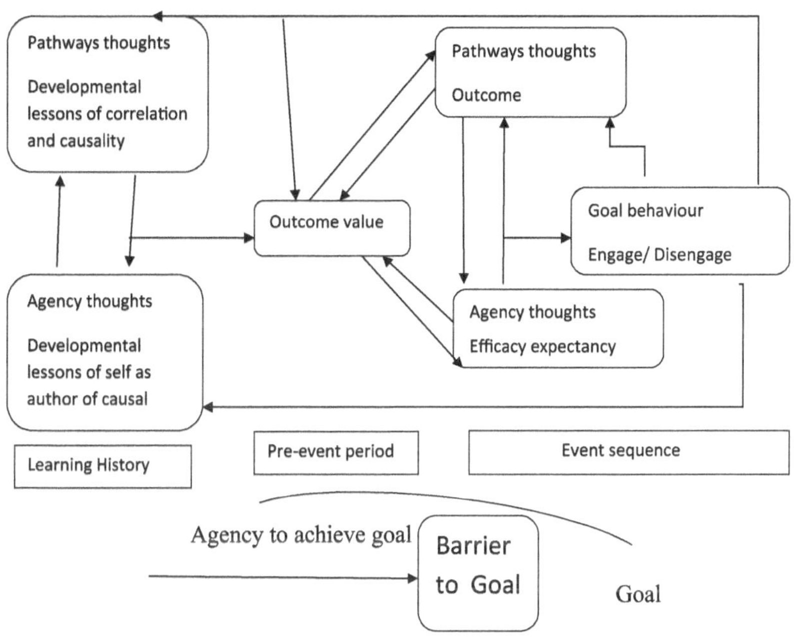

Snyder's Hope Theory

Source: **Snyder (2000)**

According to Snyder's view, goal-directed expectations are composed of two separate components. The first is **agency,** and it reflects someone's determination that goals can be achieved. The second is identified as **pathways;** the individual's belief that successful plans can be generated to reach goals. Hope is not genetically determined but an entirely learned, deliberate way of thinking (Snyder, 1994).

Agency is the will power that provides the energy and determination to persist in the pursuit of personally important goals. **Pathways are the confidence** that routes to desired goals and if obstacles are encountered;

alternative routes can be found. Hope is important because it can make the present moment less difficult to bear. When we believe that tomorrow will be a better day, we can bear a hardship today. Hope is a beautiful thing. It gives us peace and strength, and keeps us going when all seems lost. When we accept what we cannot change, it does not necessarily mean that we have given up on hope. It just implies that we have to focus our hope on more humanly tangible and attainable goals. Optimism is an expectation of the future, but hope is a way of experiencing the present. Hope is being able to see that there is light despite all of the darkness. Hope can be a powerful force. There may not be any actual magic in it, but when you know what you hope for most and hold it like a light within you, you can make things happen almost like a magic. It is, therefore, said that what oxygen is to the lungs; hope is to the meaning of life. Hope is being able to see that there is light despite all of the darkness. It is like the sun, which, as we journey towards it, casts the shadow of our burden behind us. Optimism is the faith that leads to achievement. Nothing can be done without hope and confidence. Hope is a renewable option; when it gets exhausted, it can be renewed once again. Hope is a feeling of optimism, a thought that says things will improve, it won't always be charmless, and there is a way to rise above the present circumstances. Hope is an internal awareness that you do not have to suffer forever. There is a remedy for despair that you will come upon somehow if you can only maintain this expectancy in your heart.

Optimism is a mental attitude that interprets situations and events as being best (optimized), meaning that in some way for factors that may not be fully comprehended, the present moment is in an optimum state. A commonly used idiom to illustrate optimism versus pessimism is a glass with water at the halfway point; where the optimist is said to see the glass as half full, the pessimist sees the glass as half empty. The word **optimism** is originally derived from the Latin word **optimum**, meaning **best.** Being optimistic, in the typical sense of the word, ultimately means one expects the best possible outcome from any given situation. This is usually referred to as **dispositional optimism**. Optimism is a belief or hope that the outcome of some specific endeavour will be positive, favourable, and desirable. It thus reflects a belief that future conditions will work out for the best. Optimists emerge from difficult circumstances with less distress than pessimists. Tiger (1979) defined optimism as a, "a mood or attitude associated with an expectation about the social or material future, one which the evaluator regards as socially desirable, to his/ her advantage or for his/ her pleasure". An important implication of this definition is that there can be no single or objective optimism, at least as characterized by its content, since what is considered optimism depends on what the individual regards as desirable. Optimism is an attitude reflecting a belief or hope that the outcome of specific endeavours, in general, will be positive. Contemporary approaches treat it as a cognitive characteristic i.e. a goal, an expectation, or a causal attribution which is sensible so long as we remember that the belief in question concerns future occurrences about which individuals have strong feelings. Taylor (1989) proposed that the pervasive tendency to see oneself in the best possible light is a sign of well-being. The strongest statement that optimism is an inherent aspect of human nature is found in Tiger's (1979) book, "**Optimism: The Biology of Hope**". Tiger even hypothesized that optimism drove human evolution; since it requires thinking about the future, i.e. when people began to think ahead. By this view, optimism is inherent in our own make up, not a derivative of some other psychological characteristic. Optimism is characterized as easy to think, easy to learn, and pleasing that modern evolutionary psychologists describe as an **evolved psychological mechanism** (Buss, 1991). **First**, optimism is a source of motivation. It is much easier to initiate action when we believe our actions will lead to positive outcomes. In the face of disappointment, optimism energizes continued action, while pessimism may lead to giving up. By interpreting bad events as temporary and limited to specific situations, optimists protect themselves from strong negative emotional reactions that might undermine confidence and interfere with effective coping (Carver & Scheier, 2002). **Second**, the connection of optimism to more effective coping is a way in which optimism works. Optimists are better at dealing with stress. They use active coping strategies in confronting and solving problems. **Third,** the advantage of optimism is flexibility in the use of different coping approaches. Based on the review of dispositional optimism and coping research, Ness and Segerstrom (2006) suggest that optimists distinguish between controllable and uncontrollable life stressors and adjust their coping strategies appropriately. When faced with a life-threatening illness, optimists shift their coping style from active problem-solving to more emotion-focused coping based on acceptance of reality that cannot be changed. Emotional coping involves finding ways to reduce and manage the emotional consequences of stressful events and conditions. **Fourth,** optimists enjoy the benefits derived from positive emotion. These benefits enhance **resilience** in the face of distress, social support and immunity to fight disease. Optimists seem intent on facing problems and taking active and constructive steps to solve their problems whereas pessimists are more likely to give up their effort to attain their goals. A significant positive relation emerges between optimism and coping strategies based on social support. Optimism exerts an indirect influence on the quality of life through the help of specific coping strategies. There is evidence that optimists live a higher quality of life compared to those with low levels of optimism. Optimism may significantly influence mental and physical well-being by the promotion of a healthy life style as well as by adaptive behaviours and cognitive responses associated with greater flexibility and problem-solving capacity. The term 'optimism' embraces two closely correlated concepts: the first is the **inclination to hope,** while the second concept refers to the tendency to believe that we live in **the best of all possible worlds.** Optimists are positive about events in daily life and tend to have more frequently protective attitudes. They are more resilient to stress and are inclined to use more appropriate coping strategies. Optimists believe that positive events are more stable and frequent than negative ones. They think that they can avoid problems in daily life and prevent them from happening, and, therefore, they can cope with stressful situations more successfully than pessimists. When these strategies cannot be enacted, optimists resort to adaptive strategies like acceptance, humour and positive reassessment of the situation. Through an adaptive management of personal goals and development and by using active coping tactics, optimists are significantly more successful than pessimists in aversive situations and achieved life goals.

Scheier and Carver (1985) theorized the disposition towards optimism in their studies, called dispositional optimism. Considering it a trait of an equilibrated personality that influences the way in which individuals come to terms with present, past and future events in life. This definition states that a confident individual looking at life in a positive way can potentially experience a brighter life. The way you look at life can determine your success. Therefore, it is always wise to look at the brighter side of life with an optimistic attitude. Optimism is the faith that leads to achievement. Nothing can be done without hope and confidence. The optimist sees the rose and not its thorns. The pessimist stares at the thorns, unaware of the rose. A pessimist sees the difficulty in every opportunity; an optimist sees the opportunity in every difficulty. Optimist means better than reality; pessimism means worse than reality. It is the hopeful, light hearted, cheerful attitude of mind that wins. Optimism is a success builder, pessimism is an achievement killer. The optimism turns the impossible into the possible; the pessimist turns the possible into the impossible. Optimists hope for the best and believe that everything is going to be fine in the end which helps to reduce stress. We should reinforce in our mind that everyday is the best day in the year. Optimism makes life happier and meaningful. Optimism with some experience is much more energizing than plain old experience with a certain degree of distrust of other's motives. Right attitude of human being can convert a negative stress into a positive one. Carver and Scheier (1990) identified optimism as **cognitive, emotional and motivating**. According to them a confident individual looking at life in a positive way can potentially experience a brighter life. The impact that optimism can have on an individual combined with positive illusions affect in a positive way on personal well-being. Thus, we can cultivate a positive perspective with a more cheerful outlook on life and can enhance our well-being.

Optimism and Health

Optimism, in general, has been shown to predict good health as measured by self-report ratings of general health made by the physicians; the number of visits to the doctor, survival time after heart attack, immune system functioning and longer life. Further, optimism is found to correlate with a number of positive health behaviours which influence their immunity to diseases. Pessimists tend to be loners, and social isolation is a reliable predictor of poor health, general distress and dissatisfactions with life. Another simple way in which optimism and health might be related happens to be a direct behavioural mechanism. Optimism may set into motion certain behaviours that lead to health benefits. Optimists engage in higher levels of **problem-focused coping** and **lower levels of avoidance coping**, such as ignoring problems (Scheier, Winetraub, & Carver, 1986). Optimists are better at coping and, experience less stress than pessimists.

Optimism and emotional well-being: Optimists enjoy more of emotional well-being which is considered as the capacity to live a full and creative life, and the courage to deal with life's inevitable challenges. Moreover, people who are mentally healthy can deal with difficult situations in a better manner while maintaining a positive attitude. Such people remain focused, flexible and creative at all times. Many studies confirmed that optimists tend to use coping strategies that focus on the problem more frequently compared to pessimists. When these strategies fail to work out, optimists stick to adaptive strategies that focus on the emotional aspects, i.e. acceptance, humour and positive reassessment of the situation. It is found that optimist patients adapt better to stressful situations in severe pathological conditions with positive attitude towards life. Dianne (2010) describes a person as emotionally healthy as one who exhibited flexibility and adaptability to different circumstances, has a sense of meaning and affirmation in life as well as an understanding that the 'self' is not the centre of the universe. He has the compassion and the ability to be unselfish, along with increased depth and satisfaction in intimate relationship. Virtually nothing is impossible in this world if we maintain a positive attitude. It is a wonderful thing to be optimistic. It keeps us healthy and resilient. It so happens that when we surround ourselves with positive people, we tend to become a positive person. We must discipline and take conscious effort to think positively. When our mind is disciplined to see the good in every situation, we get positive energy from our surroundings. Positive synergy can only be achieved through positive mind-set which gives a more hopeful outlook and belief that you can do something great. Inspiration comes from within us. One has to be positive. When we are able to take control of our attitude, we take control of our life. The following attributes are linked to optimism:

- Sociability: Warm, satisfying and positive relations with others.
- Positive Self-talk: Positive identity, high self-esteem.
- Positive emotion: Integrity, empathy.
- Positive reappraisal: Reframing in a positive way.
- Self-efficacy: Can-do attitude, believing in one's own skills, talent and capabilities.

Studies carried out by Peterson and Seligman (1987) stated that optimism as an **attributional style** is characterized by the tendency to believe that negative events are not constant and it will not repeat itself. Hence, optimists believe that positive events are more stable and frequent than negative ones. Within optimism we distinguish between two types of optimism: big optimism and little optimism. **Little optimism** reflects specific expectations about positive outcomes and **Big optimism** has generalized larger expectancies with positive outcomes (Peterson, 2006). A positive attitude causes a chain reaction of positive thoughts, events and outcomes. It acts as a catalyst and it sparks extraordinary results. When we are enthusiastic about what we do, we feel the positive energy. Successful people maintain a positive focus in life no matter what is going on around them. They stay focused on their past successes rather than their past failures. It is always wise to surround ourselves with positive people who believe in us and maintain distance from negative people who try to undermine our self-esteem. We should never stop dreaming, never give up, never stop trying and never stop learning. When we are positive, it not only makes us feel better, but it also makes those around us feel better. We have to live our life and to enjoy our life in a meaningful way. There are so many positive things happening around us. We must consciously inculcate positive attitude which generates and encourages the following qualities.

- Personal growth: Continued development, self-renewal.
- Goal- directed behaviour: Goal setting, planning.
- Positive thinking: Positive expectation, self-confidence.
- Self-acceptance: Awareness of one's strengths and weakness.

Optimism inspires, energizes, and brings out our best. It directs the mind towards possibilities and helps us think creatively. It is not that optimism solves all of life's problems; it can, however teach us coping with the present issues. When we have a positive attitude and constantly strive to give our best effort, eventually we will overcome our immediate problems and find ourselves ready to face greater challenges. Life is about accepting the challenges along the way, choosing to keep moving forward, and savouring the journey. The worst times can be the best when we think with positive energy.

Positive Illusions and Mood

Optimism produces positive moods and acts as a motivating tool. The mood that is experienced can influence how individuals view their lives. The way we process information can be altered depending on the mood being experienced and this can affect our thoughts. When a positive mood is encouraged over a period of time then access to positive emotions is inevitable (Buckworth & Dishman, 2002) and experiencing positive illusions can become a natural occurrence (Taylor & Gollwitzer, 1995). **Positive illusions** involve individuals viewing themselves in a positive way, and mentally healthy people do this very well. However, this personal view can lead to biased behaviours to enhance the personal quality of life and can lead to a distorted reality that may be harmful. When an individual has a distorted view then this will influence his decision making and connection with reality. Taylor's work suggests that most people maintain a positive outlook even when facing stressful events. It is a fact that some amount of optimism may be built into human nature as a basic requirement of life. When our view of life is too close to reality, all the pain and sufferings in the world may become very depressing. Research suggests that people have a **self-serving view of themselves** as better than average compared to other people. We tend to think we are more competent and more popular than other people and describe ourselves primarily in positive terms. Second, people are **unrealistically optimistic** and see rosy future for themselves in which many good things and few bad things will happen. Third, most of us **exaggerate the amount of control** we have over our lives. Fourth, people often show a bias in **attributing their failures to external circumstances**, rather than to personal factors such as lack of ability or effort. This bias helps maintain a positive self-image in the face of negative and potentially self-shrinking events. These beliefs are considered illusions because they are not actually real. However, these beliefs are not very different form real facts that they give rise to delusions. It can be said that positive illusions are mild distortions in how we view life and ourselves that promote health, happiness, and coping with stress and trauma. Thinking positively will surely drive stress, pressure and frustrations away. Voltaire had said that optimism is the madness of insisting that all is well when we are miserable. Optimism is not just a mind-set, it is the behaviour. In order to carry a positive action, we must develop a positive vision. The more we are positive and say, "I want to have a good life"; the more we build that reality for ourselves. We must keep ourselves busy and practice optimism as a way of life. Positive mental attitude is like asking how something can be done rather than saying it cannot be done. We must live our days focusing on the positive side of life, in tune with our most treasured values. Then only we find that in each moment we will have so much to live for. Positivity is an attractive quality. Since positivity is so precious, it is natural that most people prefer and nurture optimism in their lives.

Learned Optimism

Learned optimism is a concept from positive psychology's founding father, Seligman who argues that we can cultivate a positive perspective. The most popular metaphor to explain optimism is the concept of **glass-half-full.** Optimism has a built-in attitude to be hopeful all the time and consider the possibilities of good things happening in life. Optimism is a mental attitude tied with the belief that all our actions will have a desirable outcome. It is a psychological capacity that affects the way we think, feel, and act combined with an everlasting positive approach towards every endeavour a person makes.

Increasing Optimism

We do not know anything about our future, leaving it largely to our imaginations. In our thinking, we may be eternal optimists imagining the perfect situation, or diehard pessimists planning for the worst-case scenario, or somewhere in between. Optimism is the characteristic of seeing the future in the best possible light and viewing oneself as having some control in achieving these good things. Optimism also seems to be related to reminiscing about the past. When we feel nostalgic, we quite often feel optimistic.. Being optimistic, we also like to think that we have some control over those good things happening. This can bring us more hope and a greater recognition of our self-efficacy. Optimism is also one of the characteristics which is related to life satisfaction. When we are optimistic, not only do we believe that the future is bright, but we have no trouble thinking of specific things to look forward to. Natural disposition plays a considerable role in our future thinking, and some of us effortlessly maintain a sunnier outlook than others. For others, it may not be always easy to look on the bright side. Optimism is fundamental to our well-being. Perhaps viewing the future as positive and ourselves as capable of creating those positive outcomes helps us take the steps that lead to a more fulfilling and meaningful life. Optimism also helps building our resilience against life stress and improves our health. Optimism can be enhanced by fairly simple means:

- **Avoid getting hung up on one thing** Sometimes we may feel like there is one specific situation or event which is holding us back. It may so happen that we feel disturbed and impatient because of such obsessive thoughts. When we resolve to let it go, it will not bother us anymore. After all, there are so many other things that need to be focused for our survival and progress in life.

- **Get over the Past** Remember that whatever happened in the past belongs to the past. One must learn from it, grow and move on. There is no use of crying over the spilt milk. In fact, if we keep recalling the past, we are the one taking it with us into our future. We should not carry any past emotional baggage to our present and future set ups.

- **Think of your best possible self** We must seek the silver lining in every challenging situation. We remember that setbacks often occur right before we reach success. We imagine that everything works out for the best.

- **Optimistic Self-talk** We should speak positively to ourselves and others and never become judgemental and negative. We must try to shift over to only positive speech as much as possible. We have to practice using optimistic words while focusing on the positive in every situation. Modelling positive self-talk is a great way to promote optimism in children. Exchanging simple thoughts about what they liked during the day, what made them feel good, and how they are planning to make the most of the next day can be a simple yet powerful start for cultivating positive thinking in a child.

- **Surround yourself with Positive People** Positivity is contagious. Positive energy can transmit from a favourable surroundings, supportive friends and loving family members. Just being around positive people can lift us up when we are feeling down.
- **Use positive affirmations** Maximum optimism can be derived from affirmations. Affirmations can be a phrase or sentence about one's positive quality that individuals recognize in themselves. An affirmation should be:

  - Personal
  - Positive
  - Energetic
  - About present time

These positive statements bring optimistic energy into our present. They are a means of communication with our subconscious mind.

Three Good Things Exercise The 'three good things exercise' asks clients to record three favourable things that happened each day for one week. Furthermore, clients are asked to write about their role in making these good events happen. Specifically, clients are asked how they helped cause the good thing (Seligman, 2012). In doing so, the client's attention is drawn away from states such as melancholy, and instead, they become aware of positive events they previously would have missed. This intervention if continued for six months is found to increase happiness and decrease symptoms of depression. The 'three good things exercise' has also been found to increase resilience in encountering difficult situations in life (Pietrowsky & Mikulta, 2012). When we inculcate positivity into ourselves, we are able to bounce back after facing failures or natural calamities.

Put away the to-do list Every evening, rather than thinking of the whole list of tasks to be done the next day, focus instead only on three major tasks for 'tomorrow' you are looking forward to. This can help you become self-confident and stress free.

Create Something to look forward to Think and plan for ways to create a pleasurable experience. These may involve activities with others, watching a movie, and even going out for a dinner.

Reminisce Spending as little as five minutes thinking and writing about a pleasant memory can improve our mood and optimism for the whole day. Common events that make us feel nostalgic are those that connect us to people, a special place, or a special time in our lives.

Visualization Helps individuals to visualize their dreams and be able to see them clearly so that they feel inspired to take steps to achieve them. It builds the desire and confidence in them.

Empathy: Empathy begins with understanding and acknowledging others' feelings. Children who are taken care of properly usually grow up to become conscious and empathetic individuals. Parents and teachers can use simple statements such as, "I would have felt the same if I were you" to model empathetic behaviour. Learning how to empathize teaches a child to understand and accept, and helps him to reflect the same during stressful times in adult years.

Music: We all love to listen to songs that can leave us feeling sentimental about the past. Choose a few songs that leave us feeling nostalgic. We must track down their lyrics. Listening to a personally nostalgic song or even simply reading the lyrics can boost our mood, feeling of connection to others, self-esteem and optimism.

Social Learning: Social learning contributes to optimism. Optimism can be acquired by modelling. We need to be attentive to the messages we receive about the world (Seligman, 1984). Big optimism brings a significant change. A pessimistic civilization cannot survive for long.

Indeed, societies make available to people countless ways of satisfying their need to be optimistic.

Benefits of Optimism: There are a number of advantages of being an optimistic person. Some of the many positive effects of optimism are based on research findings.

- **Better health outcomes-** Optimism played a significant role in health outcomes for cardiovascular disease, cancer, pain, physical symptoms and mortality.
- **Longer Life Span-** Studies have shown that optimistic people tend to live longer than pessimists.
- **Lower stress levels-** Optimists not only experience less stress, but they also cope with it better. They tend to be more resilient and recover from setbacks more quickly. They are not overwhelmed and discouraged by negative events; they focus on making positive changes that will improve their lives.
- **Higher motivation-** Being optimistic, we can maintain our motivation while pursuing goals.
- **Better mental Health** – Optimists report higher levels of well-being than pessimists. Research also suggests that teaching learned optimism techniques can reduce depression to maintain good mental health.

Hope motivates people to approach problems with a positive mind-set and strategy-set to achieve success. People with optimistic attitudes are more likely to continue working toward their goals even in the face of obstacles, challenges and setbacks.

Positive Thinking and Resilience

Positive thinking is a mental and emotional attitude that focuses on the bright side of life and expects positive results. It is expecting, talking, and visualizing with certainty what one wants to achieve, as an accomplished fact. It does not necessarily mean avoiding or ignoring the bad things, instead, it involves making the most of the potentially bad situations, trying to see the best in other people, and viewing oneself and one's abilities in a positive light. Positive thinking actually means approaching life's challenges with a **positive outlook**. It evokes more energy, initiative, and happiness. One should condition his/ her mind to think in terms of **possible** and **can-be-done** attitude. Positive thinking can be a fantastic way to relieve stress. It can encompass cognitive reframing to combat common cognitive distortions i.e. it can involve a conscious focus on the benefits of a situation rather than its drawbacks and makes deliberate attempt to back away from focusing on the negatives in life. It involves optimism and gratitude and supportiveness and can include positive affirmations as well as deliberate effort to minimize complaints and grievances. Positive thinking is based in large part on cognitive (thought-based) ways to attain a more emotionally positive frame of mind, with the understanding that when we think positively, we feel better, and with more enthusiasm.

Explanatory Style and Positive Thinking

Some researchers often frame positive thinking in terms of explanatory style. People with an **optimistic explanatory style** tend to give themselves credit when good things happen, but typically blame outside forces for bad outcomes. They also tend to see negative events as temporary and atypical. On the other hand, individuals with a **pessimistic explanatory style** often blame themselves when bad things happen, but fail to give themselves adequate credit for successful outcomes. They also have a tendency to view negative events as permanent and unchangeable. Blaming ourselves for events outside of our control or viewing these unfortunate events as a persistent part of our life can have a detrimental impact on our state of mind. Positive thinkers are more predisposed to use an **optimistic explanatory style,** but the way in which people attribute events can also vary depending upon the nature of the exact situation.

The subconscious mind accepts everything without any selection or judgement. When we feed our mind with thoughts of fear, doubt, and hate, the auto-suggestion get activated and translate those things into reality. The subconscious is like the automobile while the conscious is like the driver. The power is in the automobile but the control is with the driver. We need to re-programme the subconscious, whenever necessary. We feel depressed because we remember past failures. We have developed the habit of seeing only the negatives in each situation, without sensing that a positive side exists. When it comes to the language we use, it does not matter if we believe the words or not, the mere uttering of them makes the subconscious mind believe them to be true. It is as though the subconscious mind does not know what is true or false; it does not judge, it only reacts to the language that is being fed. Many researchers view that we must intentionally use more positive language to shape the world view of our subconscious mind. Good thoughts and actions can never produce bad results; whereas bad thoughts and actions can never produce good results. We understand this law in the natural world but few understand it in the mental world. Believing in negative thoughts is the single greatest obstruction to success. Positive thinking changes the way we behave. When we are positive, it not only makes us feel better but also it spreads positive vibes among people around us. Positivity in our life is a function of our thinking. Therefore, we must think positive and stay positive. Once we replace negative thoughts with positive ones, we will start having positive results. Positive thinking is linked to a wide range of health benefits, including

- Longer life span.
- Less stress.
- Lower rates of depression.
- Increased resilience.
- Better stress management and coping skills.
- Lower risk of cardiovascular disease.
- Increased physical well-being.
- Better psychological health.

Each and every action is always motivated by an intention, and has an attitude and behaviour connected with it. People with good vibrations make us feel at ease, whereas people with negative vibrations make us feel doubtful, worried, and anxious. When our perception towards others is positive, we see their qualities, talents and creativity instead of their limitations. There are many ways following which a person can change negative thoughts to more realistic and positive thoughts which have been discussed in the following paragraphs:

Positive Affirmations: Positive affirmations are a great way to begin the nurturance of positive thinking. Positive affirmations should be reflected in the positive present tense i.e. **I am strong, beautiful, confident, smart, creative**, etc. By bringing it into the present tense and affirming that you already have what you want; bridges the gap between desires and reality. For example, instead of telling yourself "I will have a beautiful, peaceful home", say, "I have a beautiful and peaceful home". Allowing your energy to be in the present tense brings the energy into being in the present tense, where you want your aspirations to get fulfilled.

Examples of affirmations

- I love and appreciate myself just as I am.
- My life works beautifully.
- I am strong and healthy.
- My life is blossoming in total perfection.
- Everything is happening for my good.
- I love having plenty of energy.
- I deserve the best and accept the best now.
- I prosper wherever I turn.
- I value who I am.
- I love and cherish all aspects of myself.
- I radiate health through every cell and system in my body.
- I have the courage and self-confidence necessary to put my ideas into practice.
- I honour myself and treat myself with respect.
- I am the prime decision maker in my life.
- I trust my feelings and unconscious thoughts.
- I accept responsibility for all decisions I make in life.
- I treat each new problem I encounter as a new door to be opened, and an opportunity to be creative.
- I love creating joyful and creative relationships.
- Beautiful things are happening in my life every day.

Finally, I deserve the best and it is time to accept it now. I love myself enough to accept as I am.

Ideals versus Problems: Talking about our problems is our greatest addiction. We must break this habit and think of our ideals not problems. We very often focus our energy on our problems or limitations. However, by doing so, we put our attention on the negative aspects. This reminds and reinforces our grievances upon things which we do not want or simply we try to avoid consciously. Instead, we should introspect and analyse our own ideal vision or concept. There are three important advantages of focusing on **ideals versus liabilities**. First, we start thinking about **possibilities** rather than limitations. Second, we get a **clear picture** of what we want that helps us in achieving our ideal life. Third, by thinking of our ideal vision, we enter a **positive mental state**, which makes it easier to address challenges in our way. It does not necessarily mean that we do not pay attention to our problems and live under the illusion that as if they do not exist. It is rather the action taken by us that we are not allowing ourselves to be disturbed by problems. Moreover, we become mindful and keep our mental balance while encountering the challenges of life.

Expression of Gratefulness: We should be grateful for what we already have. We must start each day with a positive thought and a grateful heart. We believe that life is worth living, and our belief helps make it so. We are thankful for everything that happens in our life as all are our experiences. First and foremost we should love ourselves by focusing on our strengths not weaknesses. Every morning we have a new opportunity to become a happier version of ourselves.

Selective perception: We all know that every dark cloud there is a silver lining. No matter how dreadful a situation is, there is always a solution. Every problem comes with its set of possible solutions and opportunities. It is up to the person to identify the silver lining. Living a purposeful life with inspiring goals paves the way for positivity. We must concentrate and utilize the opportunities that exist in our everyday life. The difference between an obstacle and an opportunity lies in our attitude. Every opportunity has a difficulty, and every difficulty has an opportunity. A positive attitude can help us perceiving reality in a benign form. Those who can keep positive attitude in the face of tough times become an inspiration for everyone else. Hence, positivity is an attractive personality trait.

Do not think 'what if', but 'next time': Many of us like to say 'what if' when things do not go in the expected desirable direction. **'What if I had done this instead?'** This mode of thinking is neither useful nor constructive since the incident has already passed. We should rather think and say to ourselves that what can be done so that this will not be repeated next time. We learn from our experience and we also learn from others. We can prevent the same problem from happening or taking different means to bring out something different. We can see that the former approach is stuck in the past while the latter approach is a forward-looking thinking. It may happen that difficult roads often lead to beautiful destinations. Being **positive** or **negative** are habits of thoughts that have a very strong influence on life. Positive thinking evokes more energy, initiative, and happiness. However, simply positive thoughts are not enough. There have to be accompanying positive feelings and positive actions which lead to long lasting positive results.

Positive Reappraisal: This is a cognitive strategy that reframes the problem in the positive way by comparing the same with probable worse situations. The event at hand is perceived to be the best that could have happened. The human mind is amazing. The fear of being mocked because of sub-standard performance discourages us to think differently or try out something new. Again, we get inhibited in expressing our mental state and thought process. The need for social approval is an important motivating factor in human behaviour and that there is a general disposition on the part of individuals to seek favourable evaluation from others (Patnaik, 1988). In one way or another, everyone is looking forward for a sense of feeling at peace with ourselves. Psychologically healthy people have positive attitudes toward themselves and others which affect their thinking process. Positive thinking can be truly beneficial for our well-being under the following assumptions:

- Accepting and expecting positive change.
- Gracefully accept endings; each completion brings a greater beginning.

- Live in the 'present'.
- Assume that everything is all right at a deeper level.
- Choose a goal as per your choice.

Positive thoughts can increase will power and determination. Determination and willpower can make a person with average intelligence and skills into a successful person. Each and every action is always motivated by a goal and it is our thoughts that lead to action. According to the nature of the goal and the accompanying attitude with which we carry out a particular action, the output is determined i.e. beneficial, neutral or negative. A person with a good vibration and a balanced healthy personality thinks in a positive manner. On the other hand, a person with a negative bent of mind is loaded with negative thoughts like anger, hatred and guilt. When our perception towards others is positive; we see their good qualities, values and talents instead of their defects. On the contrary, when our intention is negative at the outset, we cannot be satisfied or impressed by others' goodness or generosity. Qualities like emotional intelligence (EQ), self-acceptance, creativity and sociability are considered to be the pre-requisites to strengthen and reinforce positive thinking for our mental health and well-being.

Resilience Human resilience is the foundation of well-being. Resilience refers to human's amazing ability to bounce back and even thrive in the face of life challenges. Such challenges have the potential to obstruct normal development and undermine healthy functioning. Mastein (2001) defines resilience as "a class of phenomenon characterized by good outcomes in spite of serious threats to adaptation or development". Ryff and Singer (2003) define resilience as "maintenance, recovery, or improvement in mental or physical health following challenges". Resiliency is something that occurs quite naturally. Our genetic endowment makes us capable of quickly picking ourselves up after a calamity ad moving on to the next challenge. Henry (1999) defined resilience as, "the capacity for successful adaptation, positive functioning, or competence despite high risk, chronic stress, or prolonged or severe trauma". Resilient responses to adversity are common across the life span. We all encounter a variety of challenges as we journey through life. Raising kids, divorce, relocation, job loss, illness, loss of a significant other and physical declines late in life are all common in human life journey. Researchers studying adult development and the aging process have focused on how people maintain their health and well-being and continue to grow as individuals despite the inevitable challenges of life.

Resilience is most likely to differ from one person to another. It appears that resilience is made up of different mixtures of dispositional and situational factors.

Life is never perfect. As much as we wish things would just go our way, difficulties are inevitable and we all have to deal with them. Resilience theory argues that it's not the nature of adversity which is important; but most important is how we deal with adversity. Some people seem to quickly bounce back from personal failures and setbacks, while others find it much more difficult to revive their strengths. We know that resilience is the ability to recover from setbacks and adapt to challenging circumstances and is required to thrive and flourish. It is a classic psychological tool that empowers us to feel effective and capable of handling uncertainty. Emotional resilience enables us to calm our frantic mind after encountering a negative experience. It is intrinsic motivation, an inner force by which we can hold ourselves through all the downsides of life. Resilience is the process of being able to adapt well and bounce back quickly in times of stress. Building resilience is an important part of growth and change. There are several ways to cultivate and inspire resilience in people. A good start is finding a sentence that resonates with you. It empowers you, motivates you and gives you lot of positive energy to move on. Most of us have witnessed people confronting the loss of a loved one, a serious accident or health condition, divorce of married couple or the end of a close relationship. Some people become impatient and frustrated by life's challenges and distress. They suffer significant symptoms of emotional depression and despair. They cannot tolerate adverse life events and lose their self-confidence. On the contrary, there are people who maintain their cool and hope in the equally challenging and adverse state because of their high resiliency. Resilience has been frequently associated with positive emotions especially during adverse challenging life events.

Enhancing Resilience in Childhood

Personality factors:
- Good intellectual and problem-solving abilities.
- An easy-going temperament and a personality that can adapt to change.
- A positive self-image and personal effectiveness.
- An optimistic outlook.
- Ability to regulate and control emotions and impulses.
- Personal talents.
- A healthy sense of humour.

Factors within the family:
- Close relationships with parents or other primary caregivers.
- Warm and supportive parenting that provides clear expectations and family values.
- An emotionally positive family with minimal conflict between parents.
- A structured and organized home environment.
- Parents who are financially stable.

Protective factors within the community:
- Living in an enriched neighbourhood.
- People in the community address problems and promote community spirit.
- Living in a safe neighbourhood.
- Easy availability of competent and emergency services.

Enhancing Resilience in Adulthood

Many of the factors that contribute to resilient responses in childhood also contribute to adult resilience. When we learn to become resilient, we also condition ourselves to embrace the beautifully broad spectrum of the human experience. Resilience does not mean that we remain aloof and indifferent. Rather, it implies that we experience, we feel, we fail, we hurt, we fall, but, we must keep going. The following six major factors contribute to resilience in adult life.

Self-Acceptance: Person with self-acceptance has a positive attitude towards himself/ herself and accepts all the multiple aspects of self, including strengths and weaknesses. Such a person feels positive about life. Resilience is accepting the new reality, without being judgemental.

Personal Growth: Personal growth refers to a person's feelings of continued development and effectiveness, and openness to new experiences and challenges. It is exhibited by a person who is still excited about life and learning new things. Building resilience is an important part of growth and change.

Purpose in life: Purpose in life implies that we have goals and beliefs that give direction to our life. Life has meaning and purpose when we feel that we are relevant for our family and society by our positive contribution.

Environmental Mastery: Mastery refers to a feeling of competence and the ability to manage complex environment. Mastery is reflected in a person's ability to create a suitable living space, successful management of professional and personal life, family, health, and all other conditions necessary for a secured life. Resilience is multi-dimensional. It is a variety of skills and coping mechanisms. Persistence and resilience are reinforced when one works through difficult times.

Autonomy: People with autonomy are comfortable with self-direction, taking initiative, and working independently. Such people possess internal standards that guide their actions and allow them to resist negative social pressures from others.

Positive Relations with others: People who have positive relations and warm, satisfying, and trusting interactions with others are capable of developing empathy and intimacy. Good friends, satisfying marriage and healthy supportive relationships with others help in increasing resiliency at the time of adversity. Resilience is based on compassion for ourselves as well as compassion for others.

Small seeds are equipped with potent power to push through solid ground and become big tree to give shelter to others under its shade. Likewise, human beings are all blessed with unseen reserves of great strength to face the unpredictable and unwelcome events of life.

Emotional Intelligence

Intelligence is the aggregate or global capacity of the individual to act purposefully, think rationally, and deal effectively with the environment. It is the ability to learn from one's experiences, acquire knowledge and use resources effectively in adapting to new situations or solving problems. Hence, intelligence is the skill to understand, act, interpret and predict the future and to achieve and handle relationships, information, concepts and abstract symbols. The concept of emotional intelligence as a psychological theory was first developed by Salovey and Mayer (1990) while they studied the link between emotions and thought. **Emotional intelligence** was popularized and expanded after the publication of Goleman's book "**Emotional Intelligence**" in 1995. When Salovey and Mayer introduced the term emotional intelligence, they described it as a form of **social intelligence** that involves the ability to monitor one's own and others' feelings and emotions, discriminate among them, and use this information to guide one's thinking and action. Emotional intelligence refers to the ability to perceive, control, and evaluate emotions. It is an assortment of non-cognitive skills, capabilities and competencies that influence person's ability to succeed in coping with environmental demands and pressure. The ability to express and control emotions is essential, but so is the ability to understand, interpret, and respond to the emotions of others. It is very important to understand that emotional intelligence is not the opposite of intelligence; it is not the victory of heart over head. It is in fact the unique intersections of both. Emotional intelligence is a way of recognizing, understanding, and choosing how we think, feel, and act. It shapes our interactions with others and our understanding of ourselves. It defines how and what we learn; it allows us to set priorities and it guides our daily actions. Researchers suggest that there are four levels of emotional intelligence including emotional perception, the ability to reason using emotions, the ability to understand emotions, and the ability to manage emotions.

Perceiving emotions: The first step in understanding emotions is to perceive them accurately. In many cases, this might involve understanding nonverbal signals such as body language and facial expressions.

To understand emotion, we need to clarify three terms:

- Affect- It covers a broad range of feelings that people experience.
- Emotion- Emotions are intense feelings that are directed at someone or something.
- Moods- Moods are feelings that tend to be less intense than emotions and which lacks a contextual stimulus.

Reasoning with emotions: The next step involves using emotions to promote thinking and cognitive activity. Emotions help prioritize what we pay attention and react to; we respond emotionally to things that attracts our attention.

Understanding: The emotions that we perceive can carry a wide variety of meanings. When someone is exhibiting intense behaviour, it must be assumed that the emotion is anger.

Managing emotions: The ability to manage emotions effectively is a crucial part of emotional intelligence. Regulating emotions and responding appropriately are all important aspects of emotional management.

Goleman (1995) stated that emotions play an important role in everyday life and that people can enhance their emotional competency. Goleman's five emotional competencies are:

- The ability to identify and name one's emotional states and to understand the link between emotions, thought and action.
- The capacity to manage one's emotional states to control emotions or to shift undesirable emotional states to more adequate one.
- The ability to enter into emotional states associated with a desire to achieve and be successful.
- The capacity to read, be sensitive to, and influence other people's emotions.
- The ability to enter and sustain satisfactory interpersonal relationships.

Emotional intelligence is a cluster of traits/ abilities relating to the emotional side of life. Emotional intelligence encompasses five components:

1. **Self-awareness:** Recognizing your emotion and their effects, knowing your strengths and limitations and having a strong sense of your capabilities and self-worth.
2. **Self-Regulation:** Managing your mood by keeping disruptive emotions and impulses in check and channelizing your feelings and resources to enhance your performance and productivity.
3. **Self-Motivation:** Knowing how to use your emotions toward a desired goal and to persevere despite obstacles and setbacks.
4. **Empathy:** Your ability to sense others' feelings and perspectives, read and understand the dynamics of relationships and anticipate, recognize and meet key constituents needs.
5. **Social Skills:** It refers to proficiency in managing relationships and building networks. It is an ability to find common ground and build rapport.

A cluster of traits or abilities relating to the emotional side of life-abilities such as recognizing and managing one's own emotions, being able to motivate one self and one's impulses, recognize others' emotions and handling interpersonal relationships in an effective manner. According to Goleman, Emotional Intelligence is more important for a happy productive life than Intelligence Quotient (IQ). Individual cannot make intelligent choices when they are not aware of their own feelings. When people are not aware of their own emotions, they get confused and it is evident from their body language and facial expressions. It affects interpersonal relationships in an adverse manner since other people fail to know the underlying feelings and emotions. Therefore, it is essential to regulate the nature and expressions of one's emotions for interacting effectively with others.

All of us know that success is two percent inspiration and ninety eight percent perspiration. Being motivated to take up the task as a challenge and remaining enthusiastic and optimistic about the final outcome contributes to success. The ability to read others' mind and the mood they are in is very important in developing inter-personal relationships. It is also an indispensable quality of a leader.

Goleman (2002) favours only four domains of emotional intelligence with 19 categories described in his book **Primal Leadership**. These four domains are:

Self-awareness: Self-awareness is the emotional self-awareness which helps in self-assessment and boosting self-confidence.

Self-Management: Self-management is the emotional self-control, transparency, adaptability, and maintaining optimism.

Social-awareness: Social awareness is the empathy, organizational awareness and service orientation.

Relationship Management: Relationship management is the inspirational leadership, control, developing others, conflict management, team work, and collaboration.

Block has found the following three dominant characteristics of emotional intelligence. These are:

- **Self-assurance**
- **Optimism**
- **Social poise**

According to Block, individuals with emotional intelligence tend to have superior self-control with an ability of self-motivation. They are principled, responsible and as such life appears meaningful to them. They manage and express their emotions appropriately. They are assertive and at the same time sympathetic and caring in relationships. They have a rich and balanced emotional life. They appear to be gregarious, spontaneous and open to varieties of experiences in life. Emotional intelligence encompasses a broad collection of individual skills competencies and dispositions, usually referred to as **soft skills or interpersonal skills**. It can be the ability to detect and manage emotional cues and information. A measure of one's emotional intelligence is defined by the ability to use both emotional and cognitive thought. This measure of emotional intelligence is called **Emotional Quotient** (EQ) Emotional intelligence skills include empathy, intuition, creativity, flexibility, stress management, leadership, integrity, interpersonal skills and intrapersonal skills. Physiologically it involves the lower and central section of the brain, called the **limbic system**. It also primarily involves the **amygdala**, which has the ability to scan everything that happens to us. The amygdala helps coordinate responses to stimuli in the environment, especially those that trigger an emotional response. This structure plays an important role in fear and anger. The amygdala has a central role in anxiety responses to stressful and arousing situations.

Emotional Quotient develops throughout our life; it is not fixed. When one has high Emotional Quotient, he is able to recognize the source of negative feelings and have the confidence to take corrective actions, thus, increasing long-term happiness. Hence, people with high Emotional Quotient strike a balance between emotionality and rationality.

Goleman (1998) asserts that no gender difference in emotional intelligence exists. He admitted that while men and women may have different profiles of strengths and weaknesses in different areas of emotional intelligence, their overall levels of emotional intelligence are equivalent. However, studies by Salovey and Mayer found that women are more likely to score higher on measures of emotional intelligence than men, both in professional and personal settings.

Importance of Emotional Intelligence

When we are dealing with people, we do not deal with creatures of logic but with creatures of emotion. When our emotional health is in a bad state, our self-esteem also goes down. At this point we should be little more concerned about ourselves. Several studies have found that emotional intelligence can have a significant impact on various elements of everyday living. Research findings reflect that higher emotional intelligence is a predictor of **life satisfaction.** It is reported that people higher in emotional intelligence are likely to use an adaptive defence style and thereby exhibit healthier psychological adaptation. It is also noted that higher levels of emotional intelligence are associated with an increased likelihood of self-care and positive interactions with friends and family.

Leaders with high emotional intelligence create more connected and motivated teams. The skilled people with high emotional intelligence become effective managers. They possess the ability to inspire others. They are blessed with personal integrity, communication skills and comfort building relationships. Emotional intelligence can provide the backbone of team building, productivity and group morale. The benefits of emotional intelligence at work place can be described as:

- Better teamwork.
- Easier adjustments.

- Greater self-awareness.
- Greater self-control.
- Company's overall improvement.

Emotional intelligence can benefit the leader in several ways, viz.

- **Internal Awareness:** Decision-making needs an understanding of how your feelings are affecting judgment, productivity, attitudes etc. Leaders with high EQ are self-aware of their emotions, their weaknesses and limitations, as well as their strengths. Internal awareness is not eliminating emotions from decisions, but allows the person to work rationally. In work environments, leaders who are internally aware can easily deal with the stresses and pressures that come their way. For this, it is important to know how others are feeling, acting and reacting within the work space.
- **Self-regulation:** Individuals with high EQ are self-disciplined i.e. they manage to remain calm and do not overreact in challenging situations. Leaders should not be guided by their impulsive decisions since there are greater chances of committing mistakes out of hasty decisions.
- **Increased Empathy:** People with high EQ have a greater understanding of their own emotional states. This empathetic attitude connects them in a deeper level to their colleagues and subordinates. Tenderness and kindness are not signs of weakness and despair, but manifestation of strength and resolution. As said by Aristotle anyone can be angry; that is easy. But to be angry with the right person, to the right degree, at the right time, for the right purpose, and in the right way; that is not easy.
- **Collaborative Communication:** When the leader is able to understand and study the minds of his team members, it becomes easier to communicate and act in consonance with their needful demands. Thereby, the members feel satisfied and it becomes a cohesive group.

- **Less Stress:** It is natural that workplace cannot be made stress-free. However, leader with high EQ can manage the stress without being a victim to the situation. A leader is able to mobilize the team members in a constructive way and never internalizes the stress. Persons with high EQ can also adopt different coping mechanisms to minimize stress.

Importance of Emotional Intelligence for Benefits of Organization

- **Better team engagement:** Emotional intelligence acknowledges the team dynamics and gives equal opportunity to everybody to put forth their grievances. The most required ability in business is to get along with team members and influence their actions.

- **Improved company culture:** Leadership is always a relationship, a multi-faceted equation with other team members. A truly successful leadership thrives in a group culture of high openness and high trust. Leaders with emotional intelligence encourage stronger relationships and open communication which enhances the group spirit.

- **High performance-driven output:** Emotional intelligence encourages and nurtures the passions of the employees. We all know that when passions and profession become one, the output improves in all dimensions. Leaders are not only driven by positive energy and intrinsic motivation, they also radiate the same among their group members. Emotional intelligence helps to create a congenial stress-free work culture. The work place becomes a second home for the employees with 'we' feeling and high morale.

Human intelligence (IQ) and Emotional Intelligence (EQ) are not opposing competencies. At present, emotional intelligence is a term being used more and more within human resource departments. Emotional intelligence is given priority in the selection and recruitment procedures. The management training schools are taking enough care to nurture and develop emotional intelligence. Professional career has become highly dependent on EQ along with the academic qualifications and professional degree. It is certain that the perfect blend between meaningful intelligence and emotional maturity is a necessity and prerequisite for career building in the fast changing and ever demanding organizations of today's world.

Stress and Its Management

The **World Health Organization (WHO)** defines stress as physical, mental, or emotional factor that causes bodily and mental tension. The best way to describe stress at a subjective level is any change that makes us feel uncomfortable physically or emotionally. The most commonly used definition states that **stress is the negative emotional experience accompanied by physiological, cognitive, and behavioural changes that are directed either toward altering the stressful event or accommodating to its effects** (Baum, 1990). Stress is the consequence of a person's appraisal processes. It is the assessment about whether personal resources are sufficient to meet the demands of the environment. Stress, then, is determined by **person-environment fit** (Lazarus & Folkman, 1984). When the individual perceives that his or her resources are not sufficient to meet an environmental stressor he or she may experience a great amount of stress. In other words, stress is the **imbalance** between the **perceived demand** of the situation and the individual's **perceived ability** to meet this demand.

Individuals have a fixed tolerance level for stress. When stress becomes too high, this tolerance level is exceeded and results in physical and psychological consequences. One of the earliest models of stress is the **flight-or-fight model** (Cannon, 1932). This model considers stress as a physiological response to an external stressor and views that when we encounter a stressful situation, our body responds by releasing **adrenalin**. This reaction results in acceleration of our heart rate and breathing rate, and increased blood flow to our muscles. These physiological changes prepare us to make a response either to engage in fighting the stressor or to engage in flight and attempt to escape the stressor. Stress is the result of the situation, and our perception of that situation. This explains why different people react differently to stress. Stress is a normal physical response to events that makes us feel threatened or upset our balance in some way. The stress response is the body's way of protecting us. When managed properly, it helps us stay focused, energetic, and alert. In emergency situations, stress can save our life, giving us extra strength to defend ourselves. However, beyond a certain point, stress is not beneficial; rather it causes major damage to health, mood, and quality of life in general.

Signs and Symptoms of Stress

It is important to know when the stress level gets out of control. The most dangerous aspect is that stress invades and quietly moves closer to us without being noticed. Many a times we are not conscious that we are affected by stress and has started to take its toll on our life. Stress affects the mind, body, and behaviour in many ways and everyone experiences stress in different manner.

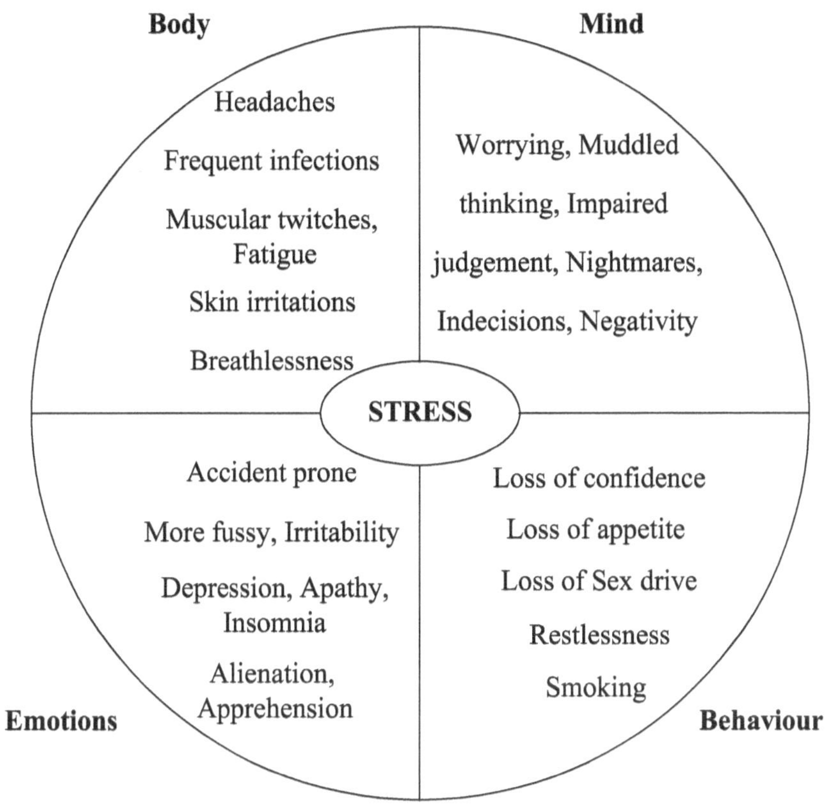

Symptoms of Stress

Physical Symptoms of Stress

- Aches and pains
- Diarrhoea or constipation
- Exhaustion, sweating
- Irregular breathing, palpitations
- Loss of sex drive
- Indigestion, stomach ache

Emotional Symptoms of Stress

- Anxiety, Mood swings
- Excessive irritability, impaired judgement
- Agitation, Guilt

- Sense of loneliness and isolation
- Depression or general unhappiness
- Feeling persecuted, withdrawal

Cognitive Symptoms of Stress

- Lack of concentration, forgetfulness
- Lack of co-ordination, indecisiveness
- Disorganized, inaccuracy in judgement
- Negative attitude, anxiety
- Pessimism, unrealistic expectations

Behavioural Symptoms of Stress

- Increased smoking and drinking
- Overeating or eating nothing at all
- Nervous habits like nail biting, hair-pulling
- Neglecting personal appearance
- Compulsive actions, neglecting responsibilities
- Isolating oneself from others, withdrawal

It is to be noted that the signs and symptoms of stress can also be the manifestations of other psychological and medical problems. When somebody is experiencing any of the warning signs of stress, it is always a wise step to consult the doctor for a complete assessment. When we take these stress-related symptoms casually, its effects may be severe and damaging in the long run. Therefore, acknowledging stress is the first step in lessening its detrimental effects.

Causes of stress: Stress does not always come from external environment. Often, stress is self-generated. This happens when we worry about things that are beyond our control, think about the past failures, and imagine the worst outcome. Stress is harmful when it becomes overwhelming. The work environment is a genuine breeding ground for stress for multiple reasons. Time pressure and deadlines are often part of a job and can cause a lot of stress. An obvious cause of stress at home is disagreement or tension among family members. Parents get stressed in raising children and for their academic related issues. Stress is compounded when parents have to bring up a mentally or physically challenged child. Moreover, family members also get stressed in looking after their elderly parents. Life changes, such as, retirement or poor health condition also become the reasons of stress. Anything that brings feelings of stress is called a **stressor**. Stress can be caused by external or internal stressors. External stressors arise from the environment and events taking place around us. Internal stressors are within our emotions, feelings and expectations.

External Stressors

- Excess work load
- Lack of insight into one's duty
- Demanding work environment
- Lack of social support
- Personal safety issues
- Lack of job satisfaction and security

Internal Stressors

- Moral and ethical dilemmas
- Feeling of frustration
- Conflict within the team
- Feeling inadequate to meet the expectations
- Poor health condition
- Unhappy family life
- Worrying about something real or imaginary
- Overwhelming responsibilities
- Times of uncertainty
- Not having enough work, activities or challenges in life
- Lack of control over the outcome of a situation

- Unhealthy life style
- Death of a loved one
- Negative emotions like depression, anxiety, anger, grief, guilt and low self-esteem

Besides all these above factors, money is a very important factor for establishing a secure stress-free life. When people face financial problems naturally their stress levels go up. In general women, elderly and young unemployed adults are affected by financial crisis. It is found that the financial crisis becomes still terrifying when there is no family or social support. Most of the factors and situations causing stress create unwanted changes and make excessive demands on us. These are perceived to be difficult and challenging to be dealt with as these stressors keep on imposing additional pressures on the individual.

Effects of Chronic Stress

The body does not distinguish between physical and psychological threats. When we are stressed over a busy schedule, the body reacts just as strongly as if we are facing a life-or-death situation. When we have a lot of responsibilities and worries, our emergency stress response system may get activated most of the time. The more our body's stress system is activated, the easier it is to trip and the harder it is to revert to normal state. Long-term exposure to stress can lead to serious health problems. Chronic stress interrupts various systems in our body. It can raise blood pressure, weaken the immune system, increase the risk of heart attack and stroke, contribute to infertility, and accelerate the aging process.

Stress and Health: Evidence suggests that stress can impact upon health and well-being. People who experience chronic stress are more likely to experience depression and anxiety. The mechanisms underlying the link with physical health are both behavioural and physiological. Research has shown that stress leads to behavioural change, resulting in inhibiting, protective health behaviours like exercise, diet, and sleep. At the same time stress promotes negative health behaviours like smoking, alcohol, and drug use. Stress can also impact upon health through physiological pathways.

The Diathesis-Stress Model: The **diathesis-stress model** suggests that some individuals are prone to stress-related diseases because either **genetic weaknesses** or **biochemical imbalance** inherently predisposes them to those diseases. During the 1960s and 1970s, this concept was used as an explanation for the development of psychophysiological disorders like depression and anxiety disorders. The diathesis-stress model holds that some people are predisposed to react abnormally to environmental stressors. This predisposition (diathesis) is usually thought to be inherited through biochemical or organ system weaknesses or acquired propensities as components of vulnerability. It is noted that whether inherited or acquired, the vulnerability is relatively permanent. The person with this predisposition is prone to suffer from stress whenever there is any type of environmental stressors creep up into his life. Thus, the diathesis-stressors model assumes that two factors are responsible to produce disease. First, the person must have a relatively permanent **predisposition to the disease**; second, this person must experience some **level of stress**. Diathesis individuals respond pathologically to the same stressful conditions with which most people can easily cope. People who have a strong predisposition to a disease may suffer illnesses even by mild **environmental stressors**. The disease results not from the interaction between personality and stress but rather from the interaction of **physiology and stress**.

Stress and Disease

Chronic stress has a significant effect on the immune system that ultimately manifests an illness. It weakens the immune system and can lead to multiple problems like chronic disease, weight gain, and heart disease. Chronic stress causes health issues which result in further stress. Prolonged stress puts our body in a continuous state of readiness for physical action. When the body has no time to re-establish it's equilibrium, it gets overworked. The immune system becomes weakened, making the individual more susceptible to sickness. Many essential bodily processes get negatively affected causing increase in health problems.

1. **Common Cold** Under the influence of continuous stress, cells of the immune system fail to respond properly, and consequently produce levels of inflammation that lead to diseases.

2. **Weight Gain** Stress hormones stimulate a preference for food that are full of sugar, starch and fat. However, researches find that the link between stress and weight gain is far more complex than simply food choices. It is viewed that the stress response produces a rise in insulin levels and a fall in fat oxidation, a dual process that promotes fat storage.

3. **Slower Healing** Evidence suggests that wound healing is slower in case of stressed people than non-stressed people.

4. **Sleep Dysfunction** Elderly people experience a natural decrease in their amount of deep sleep and an increase in night time wakefulness. Stress may aggravate these sleep deficits, making it especially difficult for older people to get back to sleep when they wake up at night. Sleep deprivation impairs memory and emotional control. Hence, people with troubled sleep may find it harder to handle stress in their lives.

5. **Heart Disease** Evidence for the role of stress as a precipitating factor for heart attack or stroke in people with Cardio Vascular Disease (CVD) is clear. Stress increases the risk of heart attacks. Feelings of depression, anger, or tension increase the risk for heart attack. Stress also increases the chances of chest pain as well as heart attacks in people with existing CVD. For women with CVD, the stress of marital conflict tripled their chances of unstable chest pain or heart attack. The role of stress in the development of heart disease is indirect but may occur through

the involvement of hormone release as a response to stress. A study that examined blood pressure provides an example of the selective effects of workplace stress. It is found that stressful situations can affect blood pressure and thus the cardiovascular system.

6. **Depression** Stress releases several brain neurotransmitter systems such as, serotonin, dopamine, and norepinephrine out of balance which negatively affect mood, appetite, sleep and libido. Some severely depressed people have permanently elevated cortisol levels, which can eventually alter the hippocampus and permanently damage brain cells. The first theory of depression is that people who can **cope effectively** are able to avoid depression, even with many stressful events in their lives. People become ill not merely because they have had too many stressful experiences but because they evaluate these experiences as threatening or damaging. They are physically and socially vulnerable and they lack the ability to cope with the stressful event. Second is the **kindling hypothesis**. This view holds that major life stress provides a **kindling experience** or **withdrawal response** which may prompt the development of depression. A negative outlook or the tendency to dwell on problems makes people more likely to suffer from depression. Third, **genetic vulnerability** is another type of risk factor for depression. Fourth, chronic **workplace stress** is related to the development of depression. Fifth, **illness** is another type of stress that shows a relationship to depression. Experiencing health problems produces stress both for the sick person and for caregivers.

7. **Ulcers and other stomach problems** The effect of chronic stress on the immune system allows the bacteria to thrive. The bacteria are able to grow since the immune system does not function properly under the influence of stress. Scientists agree

on the fact that stress can be a critical factor in irritable bowel syndrome, indigestion, heartburn, and ulcerative colitis.

8. **Headaches** Headaches are a common problem experienced by most of us at sometimes or other. For most people, headaches are simply uncomfortable occurrence, while others experience serious, chronic pain during headache. The most frequent type of headache is tension headache which is associated with increased muscle tension in the head and neck region. Tension is also a factor in migraine headaches, which are believed to originate in the blood vessels in the head and are now believed to originate in neurons in the brain stem. These headaches are associated with a pulsing, beating sensation that happens over and over again.

9. **Hypertension** Hypertension and stress are linked up because of sodium retention. Studies have found that stress can cause sodium retention in people whose nervous systems respond strongly in stress situations. One hypothesis is that sodium activates the sympathetic nervous system for some individuals, increasing blood pressure. Hence, these people experience **sodium-sensitive hypertension.**

10. **Reactivity** Some people react more strongly to stress than others. It confirms the link between stress and cardiovascular disease. This intense response is called reactivity which plays an important role in the development of cardiovascular disease. People with higher systolic blood pressure reactivity are at a greater risk for stroke that people with less blood pressure reactivity.

11. **Diabetes** Diabetes is a group of metabolic disorders characterized by a high blood sugar level over a prolonged period of time. There are two kinds of diabetes i.e. Type-1 and Type-2. Type-1 diabetes is a chronic condition in which the pancreas produces little or no insulin. Type-2 is a chronic condition that affects the way the body processes blood

sugar (glucose). In pre-diabetes condition, the blood sugar is high but not high enough to be Type-2 diabetes. Symptoms of diabetes include frequent urination, increased thirst, and increased appetite. If the disease is not properly treated, it can cause many complications. Stress may contribute to the development of both types of diabetes. **First,** Stress may contribute directly to the development of insulin-dependent diabetes through the disruption of the immune system, possibly during infancy. **Second,** stress contributes to the development of Type-2 diabetes through its effect on cytokines that initiate an inflammatory process. It affects insulin metabolism and produces insulin resistance. **Third**, stress may affect the management of diabetes through its negative impact on people's compliance with controlling glucose levels.

12. **Asthma** Asthma is a respiratory disorder characterized by difficulty in breathing due to reversible airway obstruction, airway inflammation, and increase in airway responsiveness to a variety of stimuli. The link between stress and the immune system presents the possibility that stress plays a role in the development of this disorder. Hence stressors such as emotional events and pain can also stimulate an asthma attack.

13. **Rheumatoid Arthritis** It is a chronic inflammatory disease of the joints. Rheumatoid Arthritis is an autoimmune disorder in which a person's own immune system attacks itself. The attack produces inflammation and damage to the tissue lining of the joints resulting in pain and loss of flexibility and mobility. People with rheumatoid arthritis show lower responding of stress hormone and lower levels of cortisol that healthy people, suggesting the role for stress in this disease.

14. **Post traumatic stress Disorder (PTSD)** is the development of characteristic symptoms following exposure to an extreme traumatic stressor involving direct personal experience of an event that involves actual or threatened death or serious injury.

The traumatic events often include serious injury, death, sexual assault and physical attack. Symptoms of PTSD include recurrent vivid memories of the stressful event and extreme psychological and physiological distress.

The relationship between stress and ill health is complex and multiphasic. It is likely that the relationship is affected by a number of psychosocial variables such as nature of coping with stress, personality factors, and social support.

Coping with Stress

Coping with stress is the process of managing stressors, which are assessed as demanding (Cohen & Lazarus, 1979). It is the effort to manage environmental and internal demands to return to normal functioning. This may involve approaching or avoiding the problem, changing the way a person thinks about the problem, or learning to tolerate and accept the problem. The goals of coping are:

- Reduce stressful environmental conditions and increase the chance of recovery.
- Accept and endure negative events.
- Assert a positive self-image.
- Maintain emotional balance.
- Nurture healthy relationships with others.

People constantly attempt to manage problems and stresses of their lives. Most of these attempts are considered as coping. However, the term **coping** is usually applied to strategies that individuals use to manage the distressing problems and emotions in their lives.

Coping styles: Coping styles are general predispositions to deal with stress. The two most basic styles are **approach coping** and **avoidant coping**. An individual can approach a stressor and make active efforts to resolve it, or he can try to avoid the problem. Some researchers viewed that approach coping is consistently more adaptive than avoidant coping. However, research indicates that the effectiveness of the coping style depends upon the nature of the stressor. It is observed that avoidant coping may be more effective for short-term stressors, but less effective for longer-term stressors.

Coping Strategies: These refer to the specific behavioural and psychological efforts that people use to master, tolerate, reduce, or minimize stressful events. Researchers have distinguished between problem-focused and emotion-focused coping strategy.

Problem-focused coping involves directly facing the stressful situation and working hard to resolve it. This involves attempts to take action to either reduce the demands of the stressor or to increase the resources available to manage it. The problem-focused coping is mainly oriented to do something constructive about the stressful conditions those are harming, threatening, or challenging the individual (Folkman, Schaefer, & Lazarus, 1979).

Emotion-focused coping attempts to manage and regulate the emotions evoked by the stressful event. People use both behavioural and cognitive strategies to regulate their emotions. Although, conceptually different, both strategies are interdependent and work together, with one supplementing the other in the overall coping process.

Additional categories of coping include **social coping**, such as seeking support from others, and **meaning-focused coping,** in which the person concentrates on deriving meaning from the stressful experience. People who have experienced a trauma such as loss of a loved one or diagnosis of a serious disease often are ready to realize the latent meaning at the root of the situation. People sometimes adopt spiritual means to experience positive emotions even in the face of severe stress.

Proactive coping is another coping strategy which involves anticipating a problem and taking necessary steps to avoid it. The process includes accumulating useful resources, recognizing the upcoming problems, and appraising the situation before attempting preliminary coping. It is the process of anticipating potential stressors and acting in advance either to prevent them or to mute their impact (Aspinwall & Taylor, 1997).

Factors Influencing Coping Strategies

Type of problem- Work related problems seems to evoke more problem-focused coping whereas health and relationship problems tend to evoke emotion-focused coping.

Age- Children tend to use more problem-focused coping strategies whereas emotion-focused strategies seem to develop in adolescence. It is again reported that middle-aged men and women tend to use problem-focused coping whereas the elderly used emotion-focused coping.

Gender- It is generally believed that women use more emotion-focused coping and that men are in favour of problem-focused coping.

Controllability- People tend to use problem-focused coping when they believe that the problem itself can be changed and it is within their control. On the contrary, people are in favour of emotion-focused coping when the problem is perceived as being out of their control.

Personality and coping- A person's personality characteristics provide some of the clues as to how they will cope with a stressor. Personality is defined as, an individual's pattern of psychological processes arising from motives, feelings, thoughts, and other major areas of psychological function. The way we behave, conduct, carry ourselves, the vibrations we generate give some idea about our personality. When psychologists talk of personality, they mean a dynamic concept describing the growth and development of a person's whole psychological system.

Negative Affectivity- Some people are predisposed by their personalities to experience stressful events as intensely stressful, which may affect their psychological distress, physical symptoms, and rates of illnesses. This line of research has focused on a psychological state called **negative affectivity** (Watson & Clark, 1984). Individuals high in negative affectivity express distress, discomfort, and dissatisfaction across a wide range of situations (Gunthert, Cohen, & Armeli, 1999). People who are high in negative affectivity report higher levels of distressing physical symptoms, such as headaches, stomach aches, and other pains, especially under stress (Watson & Pennebaker, 1989).

Every person is a unique entity with his own life style and coping behaviour. Some of the factors based on personality contributing to coping mechanisms are:

Locus of control- In Rotter's theory (1966) locus of control is the variable that measures the extent to which an individual habitually attributes outcomes to factors 'internal to the self' versus 'external to the self'. In other words, it is the perception that situations are caused either by some internal factors within the individual or by external situational events. Some people believe that they are masters of their own fate while others believe that what happens to them in their lives is due to luck or chance factors. The first type who believe that they control their destinies are called **Internals**. The second type who believe that their life is controlled by the outside forces are called **Externals**. It is found by researchers that Internals enjoy higher motivation, willingness and self-confidence than Externals.

Myers-Briggs Type Indicator (MBTI) (Myers, 1962): MBTI is a model of personality that identifies one's personality preferences. It is based upon Jung's theory of Psychological types and seeks to provide a model, which can help us to understand and explain differences in people's behaviour, reaction, understanding and awareness. It is a very popular approach around the world in helping people in their lives and at work. The MBTI recognizes five basic dimensions of personality, which is known as the **Big Five**, as given below:

- **Extraversion**: Gregarious, assertive sociable.
- **Agreeableness:** Co-operative, warm, trusting.
- **Conscientious:** Reliable, responsible, and organized.

- **Emotional Stability:** Calm, self-confident, secure.
- **Openness to experience**: Creative, curious, sensitive.

In addition to the Big Five traits, early research exploring the role of personality as a moderator of the stress-illness link focused on **Type-A behaviour.** Friedman and Rosenman (1959, 1976) defined Type-A behaviour in terms of **excessive competitiveness, impatience and hostility** in their interactions with other people. The Type–A behaviour pattern was perhaps the first and most controversial aspect of personality that was thought to relate stress and coping. People with this constellation of personality characteristics were prone to suffer from coronary heart disease. Early interventions helped such individuals cope better. Hence, hostility was the component that reliably predicted heart attacks. Hostility seems to be more common in people whose parents are punitive, abusive and interfering. It relates to feelings of insecurity and negative feelings about others which again intensify stress. In addition, Fredrickson et al. (2000) indicated that hostile people show larger and longer-lasting changes in blood pressure which make them feel angry. Therefore, it implies that hostility and stress reactivity are closely related.

Optimism: Optimism refers to the generalized expectancies that good things rather than bad things will happen. Optimists are the people who can always find the positive aspects of any situation and always seem to look at the bright side of life. This personality trait is associated with a number of health-related factors. Optimists tend to cope better with stress and follow better health behaviours. Further, optimism is positively correlated with problem-focused coping strategies and negatively correlated with avoidant coping strategies. Optimists, in general, possess good psychological well-being, suggesting that optimism moderates depression. Optimists tend to embrace challenges. They have a strong sense of humour, accept that change is a part of life, and believe in a higher power or purpose of life.

Mastery: Mastery is a relatively stable tendency of an individual that can influence the appraisal of stress and help coping behaviour. Mastery is defined as the extent to which one regards one's life chances as being under one's own control. People with a high level of mastery believe that they have the capability to succeed at whatever task is at hand. Hence, it becomes easier to cope when we know the nature of stress, its duration and expected outcome.

Personal Hardiness and Resilience: Kobasa and Maddi (1999) explained why some people are more resilient to stress compared to others with reference to personal hardiness. The hardy personality model grew out of existential personality theory, which emphasizes that authentic, psychologically healthy people do not passively accept their fate, but rather take control of their life. Kobasa and Maddi hypothesized that hardiness reduces the harmful effects of stress and, thus, protects from stress-related illnesses. Resilience is closely related to hardiness. When one encounters large number of stressful events but can bounce back into action, he or she is said to be resilient (Fredrickson, 2003). People are extremely vulnerable to stress when they do not know how to calm down and get back their emotional balance, which is the ability to maintain equilibrium under challenging situations.

Stress Management Strategies

Managing stress is all about taking charge of our thoughts, emotions, priorities, environment, and the way we deal with our problems. Stress management involves changing the stressful situations when we can, or change our reactions to the stressful situations when we cannot. We can adopt different strategies to manage stress.

Social Support: A strong support network is the greatest protection against stress. The evidence showing the usefulness of social support is amazing. Social support is defined as emotional, informational, or instrumental assistance from others. Social support, undoubtedly, is an effective aid to health and coping with stress. It refers to human and emotional support a person receives from others. Sometimes related concepts like social contacts and social network are used interchangeably to refer to the number and types of people with whom one is associated. The opposite of social contacts is social isolation which refers to an absence of interpersonal relations. Wills (1985) has defined several types of social support:

- **Esteem support**: other people help increase one's self-esteem.
- **Informational Support**: Other people are available to offer information and advice.
- **Companionship**: Emotional support through common interests and activities.
- **Instrumental Support**: Tangible assistance like material support and services.

The term social support is generally used to refer to the perceived comfort, caring, esteem, or help the individual receives from others. It is reported that widowed, divorced or single individuals have higher mortality rates from heart disease than married people which suggested that heart disease and mortality are related to lower levels of social support. The positive effects of social support for health are well established. The basic functions of social interaction, such as maintaining a good mood, differ in respect to its relative importance for determining social preferences across the lifespan. When people get older, they believe that they are left with limited time, which should not be invested on others who are not relevant to them. Accordingly, older adults' social net works are smaller than those of younger adults.

Relaxation Based Approaches: The great philosopher Plato had said, "the treatment of a part should not be attempted without treatment of the entirety". Relaxation training is a very important part of stress management. It provides systematic desensitization for the treatment of anxiety (Wolpe, 1958). When one can maintain calm in the face of stress, a real sense of **self-control** is achieved. When somebody relaxes, he focuses his thoughts on things that permit rest to the mind and body. Therefore, body gets time and space to clean away the toxins that have been built up during the stress-filled hours. When we do relaxation exercise, here is what happens to our body:

- Breathing slows.
- Blood pressure drops.
- Muscles relax.
- Anxiety lessens.
- Stressful thoughts disappear.
- Irritability eases.
- Stress headaches fade away.
- Clear thinking develops.
- Concentration improves.

We need to relax our body when we are feeling stressed. Most important point is how to continue with this relaxation technique.

- Find a position that feels comfortable, either sitting or lying down.
- Close your eyes.
- Relax your arms with hands slightly folded on your lap.
- Breathe rhythmically from the abdomen, not the chest.
- As you say the word 'relax' silently to yourself, focus on the muscles at the top of the head and consciously relax them.
- When you feel the top of your head seems to 'relax' move down to the eye area. Do not move on until you can feel that area is relaxed.
- Move on to the sinus area of your face and relax.
- Move to the muscles of your ears and back of your neck.
- Move all the way down to your toes, relaxing each section of your body.

Progressive Muscle Relaxation (PMR): The concept behind relaxation training is that tension is incompatible with relaxation. Relaxation exercises bring a feeling of well-being by creating a relaxed state that actually dissipates anxiety and negative stress reactions. The degree to which our muscles are relaxed can be controlled by producing a special technique called, **Progressive Muscle Relaxation or PMR.** PMR intends to induce deep muscular relaxation by gradually releasing tension from various parts of the body. These are the following points to be taken care of during PMR:-

- Start at the muscles at the back of your head and neck. Firmly tense and tighten just those muscles. Hold for five seconds, and then relax those muscles.
- It is important to keep the rest of your body relaxed while you are tensing one group of muscles.
- As you relax the muscles, concentrate, focus and visualize that muscles becoming relaxed.
- If you have trouble tensing and relaxing, practice first with your fist. Clench it tightly and then relax. This is what you should be aiming for with each muscle group.
- As you relax the muscle, imagine white light and warm energy filling the area.

Cognitive-Behavioural Approaches: Cognitive-Behavioural therapies that treat clinical disorders can easily be adopted to cope with stress. **Cognitive restructuring** can be used to replace stress-provoking thoughts. Cognitive restructuring is the process applied for finding and changing inaccurate negative thoughts that can lead to depression. Most people experience negative thought patterns from time to time, but sometimes these patterns become so strengthened that they interfere with relationships, achievements, and even well-being. When thought patterns become destructive and self-defeating, it is a good idea to explore ways to interrupt and redirect them. This is what cognitive restructuring can do. Cognitive restructuring depends on our ability to notice the thoughts that spark negative feelings and states of mind. Cognitive restructuring helps people find new ways of looking at things that happen to them. It can reduce anxiety and depression symptoms and it helps in mental health issues. There are countless techniques for preventing and managing stress. Yoga and meditation work wonders for improving our coping skills and management of stress.

Emotional expression: It is one of the most widely used forms of cognitive-behavioural therapies. A number of studies have shown that just writing out our feelings can lead to a range of positive outcomes. The best part of quick stress relief is the awareness that we can have control over our emotions and surroundings. Moreover, taking up any productive and interesting activity is a great way to alleviate emotional stress.

Positive coping abilities and quality lifestyles enhance well-being of the individual. Proper time management helps in planning and organizing activities and in reducing stress. Stress inoculation training (Meichenbaum & Turk, 1982) enables people to face stressful events with clear plans in mind. Since stress is a physical, mental or emotional factor, the physiological, psychological and social ways of dealing with stress need to be focused with equal emphasis. Relaxation exercises help reduce tension in muscles. Psychologically, a sense of contentment and a feeling of competence make life worth living. Meeting like-minded people and sharing thoughts with friends helps in releasing tension and receiving social support at difficult times. Stress cannot be fully rooted out; however, it can be managed to a great extent through the individual's conscious effort.

Mental Health and Psychological Well-Being

The World Health Organization defined health as a complete state of physical, mental, and social well-being and not merely the absence of disease or infirmity. This definition affirms that health is a positive state and not just the absence of pathogen i.e. a disease-causing organism. According to the biopsychosocial view, health is much more than the absence of disease. A person who is not suffering from diseased condition is not sick, but this person may not be healthy, either. It is important that rather than saying well-being and disease as opposite ends of a single spectrum, they are represented as co-existing. Although well-being and disease may influence each other, they can vary independently. Hence, one may have high level of well-being regardless of presence of disease. Since health is multi-dimensional, all aspects of living i.e. biological, psychological and social factors must be taken into account while examining status of health. **Feeling good** is much more than **not feeling bad** and research in neuroscience (Zautra, 2003) found that the human brain responds in distinctly different patterns to positive feelings and negative feelings.

Mental health is the state of well-being in which every individual realizes his or her own potential, can deal with normal challenges in life, works effectively, and makes positive contribution to society. The underlying factors responsible for poor mental health are manifold. In general poverty, low self-esteem, helplessness, and family pressure contribute to high prevalence of mental imbalance. Under the initiative of the World Federation for Mental Health, the first ever World Mental Health Day was celebrated on October 10, 1992. Its mission is to shed light on mental illnesses and its effects on the global population. Presently we are realizing the importance of mental health and how it is necessary to ensure our well-being.

Issues and Challenges of Mental Health

In a patriarchal society, unequal division of labour results in extreme exhaustion and stress among women leading to their poor mental health. The percentage of women suffering depressive disorder that often goes undiagnosed is close to 41% compared to 29.3% for men. Gender discrimination, demands of multiple roles that lead to role conflicts, malnutrition, domestic violence, and sexual abuse are some of the major factors for poor mental health of women. However, women who have strong family support feel secured and confident. It is revealed that men tend to externalize their sufferings through substance abuse and aggressive behaviour resulting in an under-reporting of psychological distress. The day-to-day stress of life is strenuous in its own way. Moreover, when a global pandemic like COVID-19 that brings significant changes to our day-to-day life; ignoring mental health has become increasingly more dangerous. The stress and anxiety caused by the constant threat to personal physical well-being and of our loved ones are enough to weaken mental health. With the downfall of the economy and loss of jobs, uncertainty, and emotional distress, people do suffer from a state of great confusion and mental turmoil. This ongoing crisis has triggered a mental health crisis. Throughout this pandemic, statistics show a frightening increase in the number of people being affected by mental health issues. Even before the pandemic, the statistics showed a dreadful situation with about 450 million people worldwide living with some form of mental disorder. The challenge of new realities like working from home, temporary unemployment, home schooling, and above all lack of physical interactions friends and family members has worsened this situation. In this context, the World Health Organization and the World Federation for Mental Health, urge people around the world to pay more attention to their psychological well-being. Some of the major issues and challenges of mental health have been discussed in the following paragraphs.

Identity Crisis The major challenge of adolescents is the creation of an adult identity. Identity is achieved mainly by committing oneself to a particular occupation or a role in life. Erikson (1998) stated that adolescents experience a life crisis of **ego identity** versus **role diffusion**. Ego identity is a firm sense of **who one is** and **what one stands for**. People who do not develop ego identity may experience role diffusion that leads to anxiety.

Anxiety Most of us experience moderate levels of anxiety, which is a mixed feeling of fear and insecurity. However, in some people the anxiety level becomes much higher than the expected levels which negatively impair their achievements and daily routines. For many, anxiety becomes free-floating when they face more frequent evaluations, social comparison, and experiences of failure. Anxiety Intervention Programs emphasize upon modifying the negative, self-damaging thoughts into positive task-focused thoughts.

Depression and Suicide According to Diagnostic and Statistical Manual of Mental Disorders (DSM) classification of mental disorders (American Psychiatric Association, 1994), nine symptoms define a **major depressive disorder**; at least five of these must be present during a two-week period.

- Depressed mood most of the day.
- Reduced interest or pleasure in most activities.
- Significant weight loss or gain.
- Trouble in sleeping or sleeping too much.

- Psychomotor agitation or retardation.
- Fatigue or loss of energy.
- Feeling worthless or guilty in excessive and inappropriate manner.
- Problem in thinking, concentrating or making decisions.
- Recurrent thoughts of death and suicide.

Depression is linked with suicide. In general, a sense of hopelessness, low self-esteem, and high self-blame are signs of poor mental health. In one longitudinal study, it is found that children who spend much time in watching aggressive, violent acts on Television are prone to commit criminal acts in their adult life. In addition to that, children who play violent video games experience an altered state of consciousness in which rational thought is suspended and highly aggressive scripts are likely to be imbibed in them.

Approaches to Mental Health Issues

The approaches to mental health issues can be broadly categorized under two headings: Internalizing or Externalizing.

- **Internalizing** problems occur when individuals turn their problems inward (anxiety, depression).
- **Externalizing** problems occur when problems are turned outward (arguing, fighting, and juvenile delinquency).

Biopsychosocial Approach

According to this approach three types of factors i.e. biological, psychological, and social factors interact with each other and are responsible for mental health problems. It implies that when the person suffering from poor mental health engages in substance abuse, it may be due to a combination of biological (heredity and brain processes), psychological (emotional turmoil) and social factors (relationship difficulties).

Biological factors: Mental health problems are believed to be caused by malfunctioning of the human body. Biological approach specifically focuses on the brain and genetic factors as cause of mental health problems. Drug therapy is frequently used to treat such problems i.e. anti-depressant drug is prescribed when a person suffers from depression.

Psychological factors: Distorted thoughts, emotional turmoil, inappropriate learning, troubled relationships, and stressful early experiences reinforce mental health problems in later life. Family and peer influences are especially important factors in causing mental health issues.

Social factors: Social factors that influence the development of mental health problems include socio-economic status and neighbourhood quality. It is found that poverty is a factor in the occurrence of delinquency. Research also confirms that low socio-economic status is associated with disruptive behaviour problems.

Prevention and Interventions

Mental health professionals are of the opinion that mental illness occurs from the interaction of multiple genes and other factors like stress, drug abuse, or traumatic events. These factors can influence or trigger illnesses in a person who has an inherited susceptibility to it. It is believed that depression often goes undiagnosed since many of us show mood swings, express boredom with life, and indicate a sense of hopelessness at some point of time. Thus, others may perceive these behaviours as transitory and not indications of **mental disorder**. The prevention and intervention strategies can be broadly categorized in two perspectives such as reducing health-compromising behaviours and increasing health-enhancing behaviours.

Reducing Health-Compromising Behaviours

Such behaviours include drug abuse, juvenile delinquency, unprotected sex, and dangerous uncontrolled driving. People under psychological distress, who are exposed to domestic violence and abuse fall victim to health-compromising behaviours. Specifically, adolescents are at a greater risk for numerous health problems but are less likely to receive medical interventions compared to adults or children. During this sensitive developmental period, adolescents strengthen behaviour patterns that determine their healthy progression to adulthood. When adolescents with minimal adult supervision are in tempting and dangerous situations are inclined to engage in risky behaviours. It makes them vulnerable to a host of negative mental issues (Patnaik, 2017). Moreover, many diseases and injuries can be prevented by reducing harmful and risk-taking behaviours.

Increasing Health-Enhancing Behaviour

Such behaviours include exercising, having nutritious food, getting adequate sleep, and leading a healthy life style. Research confirms that practicing health-enhancing behaviours can contribute to Quality of Life (QOL). Besides, there are other external and internal factors that contribute to health enhancing behaviours. The major external factors are social support, empowerment, positive expectations, neighbourhood, and time management. The five important internal assets include commitment to learning, positive values, integrity, social competence, and empathy. According to Patnaik (2017), besides these factors, there are also other means and steps like planning, mentoring, mastery, motivation, and above all positive emotions play a vital role in increasing health-enhancing behaviour.

Tips for Good Mental Health

Get plenty of sleep: Sleep is a biological necessity. It is really important for our physical and mental health. Sleep helps to regulate the chemicals in our brain that transmit information. These chemicals are important in managing our moods and emotions. When a person gets a good six hours sleep at night, the body and mind remain fresh throughout the day. Sleep deprivation causes depression and anxiety and the person cannot concentrate on any brain work.

Eat Well: Food intake directly affects the metabolic and digestive system and is the source of energy for the body. Right amount of calories, proteins and vitamins is very important in keeping mind and body healthy. Certain mineral deficiencies, such as, iron and Vitamin B12 deficiencies can give us a low mood.

Avoid alcohol, smoking and drugs: Excessive drinking for prolonged periods causes thiamine deficiency. Thiamine is important for our brain function and a deficiency can lead to severe memory problems. Research suggests that some drugs cause mental disorders like paranoia, delusions, and schizophrenia.

Benefits of Sunlight: Sunlight is a great source of Vitamin-D. Vitamin-D is necessary for the well-being of our body and brain. Vitamin-D helps our brain to release chemicals like endorphins and serotonin which have a positive effect on our mood. It is seen that people often get depressed in winter season since they do not get enough sunlight during this time. This is known as **Seasonal Affective Disorder (SAD)** which is mostly felt in cold countries.

Stress: Stress disturbs our mental health. It is always wise to know the roots of our stress and act consciously either to avoid or to cope with the challenges. It may so happen that when we break down our worries and stresses and write them down, we feel that we are able to manage them to some extent.

Activity and Exercise: Activity and exercise are essential in maintaining good mental health. Being active not only gives us a sense of achievement, it boosts the chemicals in the brain that help put us in good mood. Exercising can help eliminate low mood, anxiety, stress and feeling tired and lazy. It is also linked to our longevity.

Do something of your choice: We must make time for doing the things of our choice. If we are not engaged in things we really enjoy, we lose our interests and get distracted easily.

Sociability: According to **social convoy theory** people move through life surrounded by social convoy circles of close friends and family members of varying degrees of closeness. Such circles provide mutual assistance, well-being and social care, concern, and support. Positive relations with others i.e. warm, satisfying and trusting interaction with others helps in coping with stress.

Altruism: When we do good to others, we are doing best to ourselves. Helping someone can help in boosting our self-esteem and make us feel good. Feeling of belongingness to something larger than ourselves facilitates well-being. Altruism is the principle and moral practice of concern for happiness of other human beings. It is helping others at some cost to ourselves.

Promotion of Good Mental Health: To be healthy is to be empowered. Health gives life, energizes, and empowers human being. Empowerment is synonymous with positive health. Health psychologists promote physical and mental health. They specialize in how biological, psychological and social factors affect health and illness. The WHO Commission on Social Determinants of Health 2007 emphasizes the importance of empowerment as means of achieving health equity. It identifies three major dimensions of empowerment i.e. material, psycho-social and political, with a special emphasis on the disadvantageous position of women. In this context Maslow's (1970) Self-actualization need may be taken into consideration. It is the need to actualize that 'one is capable of doing'. This has got considerable relevance for the promotion of mental health. Maslow's Self-actualization principle aims at maximizing **all that you can be**. It raises the issue of whether health is an end in itself, a terminal value or it is instrumental for the achievement of other related valued goals. It is obvious that health must involve some balance between mental, physical and social components. The dynamic interaction between individuals and their environments is recognized within the definitions of health promotion as enabling people to gain control over their lives and their health. It can be summarized as follows;

- Evidence on the prevalence and causes of mental health problems.
- Promote the formulation and implementation of health policies that cater to the needs and concerns from childhood to old age.
- Seeking help from competent health care providers to recognize and treat mental health consequences of domestic violence, sexual abuse and acute and chronic stress in women.

Health psychologists develop health care strategies that promote emotional, physical, and social well-being. In real life situations, it is important to understand and practice these strategies to avoid negative emotions like anxiety, sadness, anger and despair. Every thought creates energy. We must entertain happy thoughts and feelings, thereby creating happy energies. We should deliberately choose to enjoy the present moment rather than brooding over the bad yesterday. It is always wise to bring out positive emotions in all walks of life. Positive attitude should be inculcated by appreciating simple joys in life and at the same time discarding all negative feelings. A person who is mentally healthy has the power to face all kinds of challenges in life. It is a common notion that women are mentally weak due to lack of awareness and less exposure to outside world. Hence, women can be made aware and conscious of their mental health through education, good health, self-reliance and financial stability. Sound mental health enhances harmonious development of women and enables them to complement their male counterparts. There is nothing more important in life than mental health. When one is committed to enjoy good mental health and learns to accept life as it is, then life becomes an everyday celebration.

Psychology of well-being: Well-being is the experience of health, happiness, and prosperity. Well-being includes the presence of positive emotions and moods such as contentment and happiness and the absence of negative emotions like depression and anxiety. Well-being can be described as judging life positively and feeling good. It includes good mental health, high life satisfaction, a sense of meaning or purpose, and ability to manage stress. Simply, well-being is just feeling well. Since well-being is such a broad experience, researchers from different disciplines have examined different aspects of well-being that include the following:

- Emotional well-being
- Physical well-being
- Social well-being
- Workplace well-being
- Societal well-being

Emotional Well-being: To develop emotional well-being, we need to build emotional skills i.e. skills like positive thinking, emotion regulation, and mindfulness. Often, we need to build a variety of these skills to cope with the wide variety of situations we encounter in our lives. When we build these emotional well-being skills, we can better cope with stress, handle our emotions in the face of challenges, and quickly recover from disappointments. As a result, we enjoy our lives and at the same time can focus on our goals. Some of the factors that facilitate emotional well-being are:

- Happiness
- Mindfulness
- Positive thinking
- Resilience

Emotional well-being is described as the ability to manage stress effectively. To maintain emotional well-being, one has to be resilient, and nurture positive emotions.

Physical Well-being: Physical well-being is the ability to improve the functioning of our body through healthy eating and good exercise habits.

To develop our physical well-being, we need to know about a healthy diet and routine to apply it in our daily lives. When we improve our physical well-being, we can prevent many diseases, boost our emotional well-being and minimize health challenges.

Social well-being: To develop social well-being, we need to build our social skills like gratitude, kindness, and communication. Social skills make it easier to have positive interactions with others. When we develop our social well-being, we feel more meaningfully connected to others. The components of social well-being are:

- Practicing gratitude
- Managing relationships
- Building meaningful social connections

In short social well-being is the ability to develop meaningful relationships with others and maintain a support network that helps overcome loneliness.

Workplace Well-being: Workplace well-being refers to the ability to pursue one's own interests, values, and purpose in order to gain meaning, happiness, and job-satisfaction. To develop our workplace well-being, we need to build skills that help us pursue what really matters to us professionally. This can include building professional skills and maintaining work-life balance. These skills help us enjoy our work and stay focused and motivated. When we develop workplace well-being, profession becomes our passion and each day seems to be very fulfilling.

Societal well-being: It is the ability to actively participate in a thriving community, culture, and environment. To build one's overall well-being, one has to make sure all these above factors are functioning well. To develop societal well-being, we need to build skills that make us feel interconnected with all aspects of life. We should know how to support our environment, build a cohesive community, and foster a culture of compassion, fairness, and kindness. These skills help us feel like we are part of a thriving community where one really supports one another at the time of need. When we cultivate societal well-being, we become part of something bigger than just ourselves. Although each of us only makes up a tiny fraction of a society, we all are individually responsible to create societal well-being. The major components of societal well-being are:

- Living one's own values and convictions.
- Making positive impacts on other people's lives.

Subjective well-being (SWB): Positive psychology is profoundly concerned with how people can do well, be well, feel well, and flourish. According to Diener (2000), SWB is **people's cognitive and affective evaluations of their lives.** Cognitive and affective appraisals cover how good one's life feels, how well it meets expectations, how desirable it is deemed to be, etc. **Cognitive appraisal** describes how we consider our overall global life satisfaction and our satisfaction with specific domains (family life, career, and so forth). **Affective appraisal** concerns our emotional experiences. High SWB is the experience of frequent and intense positive states (joy, hope, and pride), and the general absence of negative ones (anger, jealousy, and disappointment). When we think about and appraise our lives, we use our own standards of desirability. Then, we compare our status with others to determine our level of satisfaction, which is the subjective element of cognitive appraisal. Similarly, different aspects are associated with positive affect for different people, which is the subjective aspect of affective appraisal. Subjective well-being thus encompasses an extensive assemblage of different concepts, from our day-to-day experiences to much broader concept. It is typically considered a hedonic as opposed to a eudemonics concept (Deci & Ryan, 2008). It has mainly three distinct components:

- Frequent positive affect.
- Infrequent negative affect.
- Cognitive evaluations of one's life satisfaction.

The affective experiences and overall emotional well-being are central to our quality of life. Individuals who feel satisfied with their lives and who frequently experience good feelings such as joy, contentment, and hope enjoy high quality of life. It is proposed that an individual experiences happiness when positive affect and satisfaction with life are both high. At the individual level, genetic factors, personality, and demographic factors are related to well-being. However, the expression of genetic effects is often influenced by factors in the environment implying that circumstances and social conditions do matter in determining our well-being. Moreover, it is found that well-being is affected by life events like employment, marriage, and personal successes or failures. Some personality factors that are strongly associated with well-being include optimism, extroversion, and self-esteem. Genetic factors and personality factors are closely related and can interact in influencing individual well-being.

Psychological well-being (PWB): Psychological well-being resides within the experience of the individual. It is defined as, **the state of feeling healthy and happy, having satisfaction, relaxation, pleasure and peace of mind**. Persons enjoying psychological well-being have a healthy sense of self (Ryff & Singer, 1998). It is the accomplishment of one's full psychological potential. Vaillant (2002) defines well-being as one psychological framework that shows promise for understanding happiness and the development of one's full potential. Psychological well-being is tied to personal growth and the cultivation of one's full potential (Fava & Ruini, 2003; Keyes, 2003). The conceptualization of the well-being state is closer to the concept of mental health and happiness, life satisfaction and actualization of one's full potential. In this sense, well-being is synonymous with contentment, satisfaction with life's experiences, sense of achievement, utility and belongingness. Individuals experiencing psychological well-being have self-acceptance, environmental mastery, positive relations with others, personal growth, purpose in life and a sense of autonomy. These components can be elaborated for a greater insight into psychological well-being.

Self-acceptance: Self-acceptance reflects the realistic attitude of an individual. It is the acknowledgement and understanding of one's own limitations along with recognition of one's strength. Self-acceptance enhances growth and self-esteem. People high in self-acceptance accept themselves for **who they are**. They display the characteristics of a **fully functioning** person and attempt to actualize the selves.

Environmental Mastery: It indicates effective use of opportunities and a sense of mastery in managing environmental factors and activities, including managing one's everyday affairs. An example statement for this criterion is, 'In general, I feel I am in charge of the situation in which I live'.

Positive relations with others: It reflects engagement in meaningful relationships with others that include empathy, intimacy and affection. In one way or other, everyone is looking forward for a sense of satisfaction and contentment in life i.e. the feeling of peace with ourselves. Persons enjoying sense of well-being tend to minimize their worries and complaints, and are relatively free from self-doubt and disillusionment. People who are outgoing, courteous, liberal in their thoughts and receptive to new ideas are likely to develop positive relations with others. It has been found that having friends around in old age can do more benefits for life expectancy than having family members around. Socializing enhances networking. Networking is the building of mutually beneficial relationships (Etuk, 2006).

Socioemotional Selectivity theory: It indicates a life span perspective on how people choose with whom to spend their time. According to Carstensen (1999) social interaction has three main goals:

- It is a source of information.
- It helps people develop and maintain a sense of self.
- It is a source of emotional well-being.

By middle age, although information-seeking remains important, the original emotion-regulating function of social contacts begins to reassert itself (Fung, Carstensen, and Lang, 2001). In other words, middle aged people increasingly seek out others who make them feel good. Moreover, middle aged and older adults place greater emphasis on emotional affinity in choosing hypothetical social partners than young adults. One must invest time and energy for family and friends and maintain a gratitude diary. People derive a positive sense of well-being, meaning, and purpose from being part of and contributing back to something larger and more permanent than themselves like family, friends, social groups, organizations, traditions and belief systems, etc.

Personal Growth: Man does not like to remain stagnant; he always likes to grow into something better. There are some ways to achieve this metamorphosis in one's personality. If we fill our mind with negative thoughts the auto suggestion gets activated and translates those into reality. The subconscious is the data bank. We feel frustrated because we remember past failures. The thought which intervenes in a negative way is weakening, depressing, and even sometimes may become devastating. On the contrary vision, goals, strategies and action plans bring positivity. The most important dimension of vision is the way you choose to see yourself in your work, family, and relationships. Goals are aimed at achieving the vision. Strategies are to be formulated and if necessary may be broken down to specific action plans to achieve these goals.

Purpose in Life: Positive psychologists believe that persistence is important irrespective of the nature of our goals. By utilizing our strengths and having confidence in our ability, we can focus all our attention required to achieve the goal. In the process of our effort, we get completely immersed in what we are doing whether reading, writing, singing, or any other work of our interest. The feeling of complete absorption and intense concentration results in **flow**. Healthy positive individuals exhibit **goal-directed behaviour** and seek out a variety of experiences in their life journey.

Autonomy: Psychological well-being is usually conceptualized as some combination of positive affective states such as happiness, **the hedonic perspective** and functioning with optimal effectiveness in individual and social life, **eudaimonic perspective** (Deci & Ryan, 2008). Well-being is associated with numerous health, job, family, and economically related benefits. Higher levels of well-being are associated with decreased risk of disease, illness, and injury, better immune functioning, speedier recovery and increased longevity. Individuals with high levels of well-being are more productive at work and are more likely to contribute to their communities. As Huppert (2009) put it, "psychological well-being is about lives going well. It is the combination of feeling good and functioning effectively". Therefore, people with high psychological well-being report feeling happy, capable, well-supported, satisfied with life, and so on. Huppert also says that the consequences of psychological well-being include better physical health, mediated possibly by brain activation patterns, neurochemical effects and genetic factors.

The Well-being Models: At the most basic level, psychological well-being is quite similar to other items that refer to positive mental states, such as happiness or satisfaction. However, it is not necessary to find distinctions between such terms. When someone reports that he/ she is happy, or very satisfied with life, it means that his/ her psychological well-being is quite high. Different theories on well-being developed by researchers with the key propositions are as under:

Theory	Key proposition	Key Researcher
Broaden-and-Build theory	Positive emotions broaden awareness and enable the building resources.	Fredrickson
Flow theory	Flow is focused motivation involving single minded immersion in an appropriately challenging, goal-based activity.	Csikszentmihalyi
Hope theory	Hope is the perceived ability to produce pathways to achieve desired goals and motivation to use those pathways.	Snyder

Psychological Well-being (PSB)	Psychological well-being involves not only the absence of illness, but the presence of something positive: growth, positive relationships, autonomy, purpose, and environmental mastery.	Ryff & Keyes
Self-determination theory	There are different types of motivation for activities, ranging from those that feel extrinsic. Conditions will meet our psychological needs differently through our sense of autonomy, competence, and relatedness. In turn, this impacts our quality of motivation.	Deci and Ryan
Strength theories	Individuals have personal strengths that can be measured reliably across cultures.	Seligman, Peterson
Well-being PERMA theory	Well-being can be achieved through five keys pathways: Positive emotions, engagement, positive relationships, meaning and accomplishment.	Seligman.

Factors Affecting Well-Being

The breakdown of psychological well-being (PWB) into hedonic and eudaimonic components and Ryff's model are widely accepted theories of the structure of PWB. As far as the dynamics of PWB are concerned, it is important to recognize that to some extent, PWB is relatively stable and have been influenced by both previous experiences including early upbringing and underlying personality factors. Children exposed to moderately stressful events seem better able to cope with subsequent stressors (Kobasa& Maddi, 1999). Although baseline psychological well-being may be fairly stable, day-to-day events and experiences also exert an impact. It is observed that even the most resilient persons may eventually become very low or depressed when continuously troubled by their daily experiences. There is strong evidence that exposure to work-related stressors over long periods of time has a negative impact on PWB. Therefore, although short periods of adversity already experienced may be helpful in building resilience, long term stress is not conducive for PWB. In turn, this lower level of PWB may lead to serious illnesses, including cardiovascular disease, problems with blood sugar control, such as diabetes and immune system malfunctions (Chandola, et al, 2008). PWB theory again proposes that when the early experiences and underlying personality factors happen to be positive, these help maintain PWB to a great extent.

Well-being is a positive outcome that is meaningful for people and for many sectors of society since it conveys that people's lives are going well. Good living conditions i.e. housing, employment, and family conditions are fundamental to well-being. Advances in psychology, neuroscience, and measurement theory suggest that well-being can be measured with some degree of accuracy. Results from cross-sectional, longitudinal, and experimental studies found that well-being is associated with:

- Self-perceived health
- Longevity
- Health behaviours
- Mental and physical illness
- Social connectedness
- Productivity
- Factors in the physical and social environment

Well-being integrates mental health (mind) and physical health (body) resulting in more holistic approaches to disease prevention and health promotion. Well-being is the indicator of what people think and feel about their lives, the quality of their relationships, their positive emotions and resilience, the realization of their potential and their overall satisfaction with life. It is a valid measure beyond morbidity and economic status that tells us how people perceive their life from their own perspective. Well-being generally includes global judgements of life satisfaction and feelings ranging from depression to joy. Positive emotions which are the central components of well-being should be fostered. Although a substantial portion of well-being can be attributed to heritable factors, environmental factors should be considered with utmost importance. The correlation between income and well-being are stronger for those at lower economic levels. Studies have found that it is applicable for higher income levels as well. Unemployment negatively affects well-being both in the short- and long-term. Supportive relationships are one of the strongest predictors of well-being, which have a significant positive effect. Good health, to a great extent enables social, economic and personal development, which are fundamental to well-being. Health promotion is the process of empowering people to increase control over and to improve their health. Environmental and social resources for health can include peace, economic security, stable ecosystem, and safe housing. Individual resources for health include physical activity, healthy diet, social ties, resiliency, positive emotions, and autonomy. Health promotion activities aimed at strengthening individuals' environmental and social resources that may ultimately improve their well-being. Societies with higher well-being are those that are more economically developed, have high levels of trust, and can meet citizen's basic needs for food and health. Cultural factors like individualism versus collectivism, social norms etc. also play an important role in determining individual's well-being.

Ways to Positive Psychology

Positive psychology began to establish itself into the dynamics of human potentials and research in this field increased rapidly. Research has addressed everything from post-traumatic growth to prosocial behaviour. Positive psychology has much to offer the Counsellors from providing insight into human strengths to offering clinical interventions with a wide range of client related issues. An inquiry into happiness has evolved into an analysis of human flourishing (Seligman, 2012). Positive psychology, however, does not ignore harsh reality. It encourages an investigation into the entire spectrum of human experience including those factors that contribute to fulfilment, not just distress. Research indicates that positive psychology exercises may help increase happiness, but their influence is similar to that of positive placebos (Mongrain & Anselmo-Mathews, 2012). Yet, more studies suggest that positive psychology interventions have inherent worth beyond placebo effects (Pietrowsy & Milkutta, 2012; Seear & Vella-Brodrick, 2013).

Positive psychology is useful to the counselling field in many ways. Counsellors are more frequently employing the strength-based approach with their clients (Kress & Pylo, 2014). School counsellors (Galassi & Akos, 2007), career counsellors (Zunker, 2011), and clinical mental health counsellors use strengths-based modalities. In addition, positive psychology provides counsellors with knowledge about human strengths and their correlates (Linley, et al., 2010). Post-traumatic growth has been correlated with certain personality traits, including optimism, hope, and extraversion (Calhoun & Tedeschi, 2012). Ellis's ABC model is a significant part of the form of therapy known as **Rational Emotive Behavioural Therapy (REBT)** (Ellis, 2002). REBT explains that how one feels about any given event is dependent on the perceptual filter than strains said event. An activating event A occurs, B is the belief about the event, and C is the consequent affect. Where beliefs are based on a pessimistic explanatory style, internal attributions are made for negative outcomes. On the contrary, where beliefs are based on an optimistic explanatory style, attributions are made to external factors for negative outcomes. Thus, the nature of explanatory style determines the attribution factors. People who experience self-growth following a traumatic event perceive the event not just as adversity, but also an opportunity to protect themselves and become stronger as a result of the bad event (Blanchard, 2013). Positive Psychology offers counsellors' insight into human strengths and clinical interventions that are effective and relatively easy to administer. Hence, it blends well with counselling psychology because of its emphasis on strengths. Counsellors have been using interventions for years and the literature supports exercises such as doing good deed for others and focusing on what is right in life. Seligman developed the classification system based on **six virtues with 24 character strengths**. Clients are instructed to complete a questionnaire, available online for free that identifies their top five strengths which are called **signature strengths**. These 24 character strengths are grouped around six virtues. For example, the virtue of temperance has the strengths of forgiveness, modesty, prudence, and self-regulation under it. Once clients uncover their signature strengths, they are asked to use their strengths in innovative ways each day for one week (Seligman et al., 2005). Counsellors can use a strength-based approach to help their clients more efficiently to reach their goals. Consequently, this leads to greater need fulfilment and enhanced well-being for clients. The signature strengths of positive psychology help well to solution-focused models of counselling. Their integration has been useful in approaching anxiety disorders (Quick, 2013) Moreover, solution-focused theory and strengths-based approaches are effective in intervention programs to help clients and treat depression (Lehmann & Simmons, 2009).

In order to lead a meaningful life, one should use his/her signature strengths in the services like charity, community, organizations, and belief systems which are larger than the selves. It can give a positive sense of well-being, belonging, meaning, and purpose from being part of and contributing to something more permanent than the self. Seligman and his colleagues studied the benefits of various interventions of imbibing positivity into oneself. These interventions generated positive emotions that helped our well-being. The purpose of positive psychology practices is to develop sound theories of optimal functioning and to find empirically supported ways to improve well-being of people.

Best possible Self The best possible self-exercise has been found to raise and sustain a positive mood (Sheldon & Lyubomirsky, 2006). In this exercise, clients are asked to first visualize their optimal selves, complete with a realistic but ideal environment in which this 'self' exists. Next, clients are to record their thoughts on paper daily or at least once in a week. Benefits from completing the exercise include improving positive affect and flow along with boosting optimism (Layous, Nelson, & Lyubomirsky, 2013).

Focus on effort rather than results Seligman stressed the role of right attitude in building optimism. Positive thinkers always focus more on the process than on the outcome. Encouraging children to participate in activities without worrying about winning or losing is a great message for nurturing this concept. Parents who appreciate children for their efforts irrespective of the results are successful in raising their children to become self-confident adults.

Changing perspective A shift from negative to positive perspective can be both the cause and the consequence of optimism. Parents should make children understand that it is not possible to possess or acquire anything which is beyond their control and limits. It is a significant step to make them more practical and worldly-wise in future.

Remember that even a successful life has ups and downs Life cannot be always perfect. It has got its ups and downs with many options. One can make the best of it. We have to accept the fact that we may have to face challenges and adversities. We may not succeed at one field, but there are chances that, with will power and perseverance, we can succeed at other fields.

Self-Direction Self–directedness is a personality trait of self-determination i.e. the ability to regulate and adapt behaviour to the demands of the situation. It is an indispensable trait in order to achieve personally chosen goals and success in life. Self-direction is the continuous exercise related to the goal. It is the ability to get access to and choose from a full range of available and appropriate options.

Self-determination The individual is conceived as being endowed with his own set of needs, desires, and interests that he must satisfy to get happiness and achieve success. He must make his own destiny, find his own path, and travel independently. To maintain our own identity in a world that is constantly trying to make us something else is the greatest accomplishment on the part of the individual.

Self-Knowledge It is about identifying and promoting those modes of thinking and feeling that leads to happiness and a satisfying life. At the same time, it aims at ignoring those thoughts that bring unhappiness and discontentment.

Self-cultivation The individual sees himself as a project of improvement and growth. It is not actually about changing the model of being **oneself,** but being still better within this model. Enhancing one's virtues and strengths to achieve a constant inner refinement and a significant improvement of one's living conditions are the pre-requisites for self-cultivation. Hence, this improvement and growth are related to the development of new practices that contribute to well-being, happiness, and success of the self.

Self-accountability The pursuit of happiness, health, success and well-being are not just a 'natural' right. These are universal objective and, above all, a moral obligation. It requires continuous **self-monitoring**, **self-control**, and **self-improvement**. The individual as such is solely responsible for his success or failure.

Creating and fulfilling purpose of life We can always find our passion and live with a purpose. A happy life can always be created. One can wake up each morning fulfilled and excited about what's to come. We live each day in the context of what matters most to us. While deciding the purpose of life several thoughts come to our mind regarding

- Centre of my life.
- Character of my life.
- Contribution of my life.
- Communication of my life.
- Commitment of my life.

To discover life purpose one may also think of

- What should I do with my life?
- What is my passion?
- What is my life purpose?

These points can be elaborated in the context of fulfilling purpose of life.

♦ **Develop a life purpose statement**

We all have goals; some big, some small, some safe and some bold. Our motivation comes from within, whether it is triggered by rewards or efforts. Some time we engage in intrinsically motivating activities other than the enjoyment these activities bring us. It is in our nature to strive, aspire, and to move in the direction of our goal. Motivation is a psychological force that enables action and has long been the subject of scientific enquiry. We must take time for ourselves and create a life purpose statement. We should recognize our experiences and retrospect the times we have experienced the greatest joy in our life. We have to be curious since curiosity leads to exploration of novel ideas. We need to create a life purpose statement focusing on what really matters to us. Every experience, no matter how simple it seems outwardly, holds within it a blessing of some kind. Our life is shaped by our attitude for we become what we think.

Define your goals First be clear about your purpose and intentions. Next explore the roads that lead to your goals and the obstacles in your way. Often, these obstacles become opportunities for growth and change. Purpose is about intentions that help build the framework for your plans and fulfilment in life. Align your goals with your life purpose and passions.

♦ **Look at the big picture and then fill in the details**

We explore the things we love to do and what comes in the most natural way. We may ask ourselves what qualities we enjoy the most in the world. Parents and the society at large influence and convey the desirable behaviour and the priorities in life. These influences have got weightage; however, it is also important to follow the inner voice and guidance which is unique to the individual. When we want to live with purpose, we need to understand and explore what we value most. The easiest way to begin is to look at the big picture and then workout the small details.

♦ **Use strengths and identify weaknesses**

We must recognize our special gifts. Then we can apply our abilities to reveal our gifts and talents. At the same time, we must find out the weaknesses in us.

+ **Create Integration**

We should bring the full complement of our mind, body, and spirit day in and day out. There should be cohesion between our inner and outer life. We should accept whatever challenge comes into our life and at the same time should focus on what really matters in life.

+ **Cultivate awe, gratitude, and altruism**

Certain emotions and behaviours that promote health and well-being can also foster a sense of purpose i.e. awe, gratitude, and altruism. The experience of awe makes us feel connected to something larger than ourselves and it can provide the emotional foundation for a sense of purpose. Of course, feeling awe by itself cannot give us purpose in life. We also need to feel driven to make a positive impact on the world. Gratitude and altruism work together to generate meaning and purpose. We all know that we may not have everything we want in life, but we are blessed enough to have all that we need. We should be thankful for our struggle since we derive our strengths from challenges. The struggle ends when gratitude begins. Moreover, gratitude is strongly and consistently associated with greater happiness.

+ **Reading**

Reading connect us to people we never know, across time and space. It is an experience that research says is linked with a sense of meaning and purpose.

+ **Think about your legacy**

We should imagine what kind of legacy, we would like to leave. Erikson called the final stage in life, **Ego integrity Vs. Despair**. This reminiscence happens at the sunset of life. We reflect on our past and realize our satisfactions and our regrets. We ponder over what messages we wish to leave behind about our identities and our values. This conviction helps us shaping our deeds and purpose in life.

♦ Developing Gratitude

Gratitude is the seed that sprouts positivity. It is the foundation of positive thinking. Gratitude goes far beyond than saying 'thank you'. When we are grateful, we affirm that a source of goodness exists in our lives. It is the most exquisite form of courtesy. Gratitude unlocks the fullness of life. It turns chaos to order, confusion to clarity and a stranger into a friend. We must develop an attitude of gratitude, and give thanks for everything that happens. Every step forward is a step toward achieving something bigger and better than our present situation. According to Lyubomirsky (2009) gratitude interventions in all forms are an essential part of **Positive Psychology Interventions (PPIs)** at work. PPIs are used alone or in combination with other interventions with the purpose of enhancing self-contentment and joy. Some examples of gratitude intervention include:

- Gratitude journaling.
- Group gratitude exchange sessions.
- Sending gratitude exercises.
- Guided gratitude meditation.

Gratitude is among the most highly researched of the variables studied in positive psychology. Research indicates that gratitude is associated with everything from lower levels of the stress hormone cortisol to having higher life satisfaction (Wood, Joseph, & Maltby, 2008). It is associated with increases in relationships connection and satisfaction (Algoe, Gable, & Maisel, 2010). The state of being gracious and the general trait of gratitude are associated with increased happiness (Watkins, 2013). Clinically, one application of gratitude that has been proved to increase happiness is the gratitude visit. This technique entails instructing clients to first consider someone from their past who helped them, but was never properly thanked. Clients are then instructed to write a thank you note to this person, being as specific as possible about the deed and how the kindness affected their life. Next, if possible, the client is asked to deliver the letter in person. At this time, the client is asked to read out the content of the letter loudly. This intervention helps to increase happiness.

Mindfulness

It is a mental state achieved by focusing one's awareness on the present moment, while calmly acknowledging and accepting one's feelings, thoughts, and bodily sensations. Mindfulness pervades much of human activity. It is about being aware of internal and external stimuli by witnessing the act in a non-judgemental manner. It is enhanced awareness of present experience and reality, while being totally attentive at the same time. Mindfulness may be defined as the intentionally focused awareness of one's immediate experience. This experience is a moment-by-moment attention to thoughts, emotions, physical sensations, and surroundings. To practice mindfulness is to become grounded in the present moment. One simply becomes an observer of the arising and passing away of various experiences. We do not judge the experiences and thoughts; nor do we try to figure things out, and draw conclusions, during mindfulness. Benefits of mindfulness practice include reduction of stress, anxiety, depression, and chronic pain. Mindfulness plays an important role in detaching self from unwanted habits and counterproductive work behaviour. Mindfulness is important in dealing with behavioural regulation which is associated with well-being. Developing mindfulness can be possible through:

- Reading books of your choice.
- Writing daily diary.
- Write what you like.
- Write what is disturbing you.
- Creative writing.
- Listen to songs and music.
- Manage your time on priority basis.

When people are described as being mindful, it typically means that they pay attention to what is happening to the mind, body, and their surroundings. Developing mindfulness practice has proved to bring numerous benefits for the body, mind, and soul. Mindfulness represents an in-the-moment and non-judgemental way of responding to thoughts and feelings. It involves paying attention to something in a particular way, on purpose, in the present moment, non-judgementally. Mindfulness does not allow **rumination** i.e. the unhealthy pattern of behaviours where we continuously think about something that happened in the past. One of the most fascinating things about mindfulness is that it is a powerful practice that can be applied to almost any area of our lives. Mindfulness is the connecting bridge between our mind and the present moment. It is the art of staying aware of what is happening right now, what we are thinking about this very moment, and how we are feeling at present. Mindfulness is being aware of what the present moment offers; it is the basic human ability to be fully present. Being present in the moment is very empowering. It means focusing our awareness on the here and now. In the hustle and bustle of modern life it is more important to find ways to become attuned to our inner state and what is happening around us. We are flooded with sensory stimuli that prevent us from being fully present in the moment with ourselves. The combination of psychology and the practice behind mindfulness appears to be the perfect approaches to help people better understand how the mind works and how to put insights into practice to create a more focused life. Mindfulness is the state of mental calmness, often achieved by focusing our awareness on the present moment and accepting any feelings, thoughts, and sensations. Regular practice of mindfulness enhances our overall health and reduces stress levels significantly. Our life is what our thoughts make it. Thoughts, feelings, and emotions, which we experience every day, shape the nature of our reality. Mindfulness can boost the quality of our lives in several ways. In today's rush, we all think too much, seek too much, and forget about the **joy of just being**. The amazing benefits of practicing meditation and mindfulness are available to everyone who practices these skills. As such people who meditate regularly are happier, healthier, and more successful than those who don't.

In a simple sense mindfulness is a way of befriending ourselves and our experience. The best way to capture moments is to pay attention. This is how we cultivate mindfulness. The present moment is the only time over which we have dominion. The mind is just like a muscle; the more we exercise it, the stronger it gets and the more it can expand. The best we can do with our future is to prepare ourselves for numerous possibilities. When we start making the effort to **wake ourselves up,** we become mindful in our activities. Being mindful we can condition ourselves live in the present moment and to handle obstacles to help us live our best lives.

However, mindfulness meditation does not change our life. Life remains as fragile and unpredictable as ever. Meditation helps our perception to accept life as it is. It prepares us to live in harmony with our thoughts, words, and actions. Mindfulness is both maintenance and treatment; it essentially trains our attention to not only be aware of our own inner workings but also of what's happening around us.

Sustaining Activities and Experiences

Practical applications of positive psychology include helping individuals and organizations identify their strengths and use them to increase and sustain their respective levels of well-being Therapists, counsellors, coaches, and various other psychological professionals are using various methods and techniques to build and broaden the lives of individuals who are not necessarily suffering from mental illnesses or disorders. Positive Psychology Interventions (PPIs) to build and broaden the lives of individuals can be divided into seven categories. These are as follows:

- **Savouring PPIs**

Savouring interventions focus on a particular experience and aim at enhancing their effects for maximizing happiness. The core principle of these interventions is to encourage the person to concentrate on every little aspect of experience i.e. physical, sensory, emotional, or social. Savouring interventions can be connected to everyday experiences like eating, smelling, or observing. It needs only little more orientation and focus on what we are consciously attending to. Savouring PPIs can be reliably used for treating people suffering from depression and mood disorders.

◆ Gratitude Interventions

Gratitude evokes strong feelings of positivity in the person who gives it and the person who receives it. The target of gratitude-based positive psychology is that if you are keen to find happiness, then you have to be grateful. Gratitude interventions are categorized into two parts.

- Self-reflective practices, i.e. writing a gratitude journal that we keep to ourselves and use as a tool for self-expression.
- Interactive methods where we actively express our gratitude to others by saying 'thank you', giving small tokens of appreciation, or paying gratitude visits. Gratitude interventions have proven benefits in increasing happiness and satisfaction in life.

◆ Kindness Boosters

Kindness is a trait that all happy people possess. Studies have shown that happiness and kindness go hand in hand and complement each other. Positive Psychology Interventions focusing on compassion can be simple acts like buying someone a small gift, volunteering for a noble cause, donating something for a greater cause, or helping a stranger in need. Kindness reinforces happiness and positivity. The objective of kindness is to promote happiness through altruistic and selfless activities.

◆ Empathy PPIs

Empathy-oriented PPIs focus on strengthening positive emotions in interpersonal relationships. Healthy social bonds both at personal and professional fronts are essential for happiness and inner peace. Empathy-based interventions focus on building relationships through effective communication, broadened perception, and bridging the gap between self and others. PPI that promotes empathy include activities like self-love meditation and mindfulness practices, where individuals create positive feelings toward themselves and others by being more mindfully connected to the present. The main principle behind this is to let us understand others perspective and build a strong connection to them.

♦ Positive Affirmations

Positive affirmations like compliments are **verbal sunshine** that brings an immediate sense of pleasure and pride in us. As a PPI, affirmations redirect the mind to focus on the positive sides in ourselves and push ourselves to act positively. These can be simple statements that we say to ourselves every day. Here are some positive affirmations that we can choose to say to ourselves and let happiness fill our mind. Happiness is a choice that we should make every day.

- I deserve to be happy.
- I love my body and mind deeply.
- Today, I will reflect only on the good things.
- I forgive myself for all my past mistakes.
- I hold no grudges against anyone.
- Whatever has happened is for good.
- I will live in the present.
- From today, I will abandon old habits and embrace new and better ones.
- I am grateful for everything I have got so far.
- I am a fighter, and I will overcome any adversity.
- I will love myself more from today.
- Everything is okay and I am at peace with myself.

The Imagined Self-Technique

Optimistic interventions crate positive outcomes. An example of an optimistic PPI is the **'imagine yourself'** test where participants are asked to note down where they see themselves in the future. Imagined self is a guided PPI that involves imagining your ideal self and feeling the joy that you would have felt out of it. Research showed that this exercise acts as a catalyst and provokes people to 'enact' achieving the life they want to live and derive maximum pleasure from it. The steps in this technique are simple:

- Imagine yourself in the future, living the life you have dreamt of, with all the people you want to share it with.
- Imagine that you achieve everything that you are struggling for now, and you are proud of your achievements.
- Immerse yourself into that imagined self and try to entertain the happiness and positivity that you think you may be feeling then.
- Next, ask yourself what you can do to reach that stage in life, and journal your responses.

Strength-Building Measures

Strength in positive psychology refers to internal capacities and values. Studies have illustrated that awareness and acknowledgement of power help reducing symptoms of depression and increasing self-contentment. Strength-based PPI conveys the message that, it is within ourselves that we find the strength we need. Psychologists refer to it as, **practical wisdom** that help us to maintain ourselves. We all have the ability to make a narrative out of our own lives that gives us a framework and helps us make sense of our experiences.

Meaning-Oriented PPI

This helps in understanding what is meaningful to us in life and what we can do to achieve the things that matter in life. A person who has clear perception of goals and expectations is more likely to feel focused and contented. According to Maslow's theory of need hierarchy, the highest level of human needs include self-enhancement and self-esteem, both of which are interwoven to find the true meaning of life. Meaning-oriented PPIs include activities like finding meaning in our daily activities, setting realistic goals, and adopting effective means to achieve them. Meaning-oriented PPIs are widely used for treating depression, anxiety, and especially Post-Traumatic Stress Disorder, where a person needs guidance to cope with the after effects of a disaster. Now-a-days these interventions are being widely used in fields such as mindfulness, life coaching, relationship counselling, and in general, psychotherapy as well. In treating a psychopathological condition or guiding people to improve their well-being, PPIs target to go into the root causes of the problem. It also lets people realize the source of their problems and enlighten them to incorporate the changes wholeheartedly. The two operating factors that contribute to the success of these interventions are; a shift of attention from negative to positive and internalization of positive emotions.

It is found that cancer patients who are treated with PPIS showed improved coherence and better stress management. Meaning-oriented PPIs also proved effective for patients suffering from life-threatening critical health conditions. It is suggested that PPIs and improve our state of well-being by impacting upon the fourteen fundamental factors of happiness (Fordyce, 1983).

Fordyce's fourteen factors of happiness are:

1.   Being more active and busy.
2.   Spending more time socializing.
3.   Being productive at work.
4.   Being more organized and well planned.
5.   Reducing worries and negative contemplations.
6.   Fewer expectations and being realistic.
7.   Practicing positivity through optimistic thinking and reasoning.
8.   Getting more focused and mindfully aware of the present.
9.   Developing and maintaining a healthy personality.
10.   Being more empathetic.
11.   Being true to oneself at all times.

12.   Replacing negative thoughts with positive ones.
13.   Valuing close relationships.
14.   Thinking about enhancing happiness.

The feeling of happiness is a wonderful experience emotionally and we want to create more of that in our lives. Research studies have confirmed that being happy is beneficial on several accounts. Positive psychology has taken this concept of happiness into the realm of scientific research for establishing a better understanding of global well-being and meaningful living.

Helping Positivity

Positivity is an important aspect of life. In order to experience and maintain a state of contentment and fulfilment, we have to first realize how true freedom prevails in life. Then we learn to use it so that it strengthens and helps us to achieve the full potential of our individual self. Freedom is the key to contentment. We also need to know what bring us close to the state of fulfilment and what takes us away from it. Yogic practices enhance muscular strength and body flexibility, promote and improve respiratory and cardiovascular function. Yoga reduces stress, anxiety, depression, chronic pain. It improves sleep patterns, and enhances overall well-being and quality of life. It is the ultimate practice for our overall well-being.

Yoga has its origin in ancient India. Its methods and purposes are universal which is not based upon any cultural background but simply on the individual. Yoga, which is a three thousand years old tradition is now regarded as a holistic approach to health and is classified by the National Institutes of Health as a form of Complementary and Alternative Medicine (CAM). The word **Yoga** comes from the Sanskrit root "Yuj" which means union, or Yoke, to join, and to direct and concentrate one's attention. Regular practice of Yoga promotes strength, endurance, flexibility and facilitates characteristics of friendliness, compassion, and greater self-control, that nature a sense of calmness and well-being. Regular practice of yoga brings changes in life perspectives and self-awareness. It can create positive energy and authentic happiness to live life fully. Yoga simultaneously stimulates our inner light and quiets our overactive minds. It is both energy and rest. True yoga is not about the shape of our body, but it enriches the true shape of our life. It is not to be performed, it is to be lived. Yoga is not a work-out; it is a work-in. This is the point of spiritual practice, to make us open up our hearts, and focus our awareness so that we can know what we already know and be who we already are.

Fear is one of the major obstacles in experiencing contentment. The unrevealed weaknesses, inability to apply our virtues, lack of focus, inner instability, etc. cause negativity within us. We have to free ourselves from the influences of any of the personality traits that restrict our progress and do not allow our inner being to manifest and express with all its potentials. To live in contentment, we should be in charge of our inner mental and emotional world. To achieve fulfilment, we should have inner control, and also remain vigilant that there is no space for nurturing weaknesses in our personality. Since, if we strengthen ourselves on one hand and at the same time get weakened by some other means, we may not reach at the desired state of inner power.

Yoga philosophy and practice were first described by **Patanjali** in the classic text, **Yoga Sutras,** which is widely acknowledged as the authentic text on Yoga. The practice of Yoga produces a physiological state opposite to that of the flight or fight stress response. Many people identify Yoga only with the asanas; the physical practice of yoga. However, asana is one of the many tools used for healing the individuals. It is noticed that only three of the 196 sutras mention asana and the remainder of the text discusses the other components of yoga including conscious breathing, meditation, life style, diet, visualization, and the use of sound, among many others. In Yoga sutras, Patanjali outlines an eightfold path to awareness and enlightenment called **ashtanga,** which literally means **eight limbs.** The eight limbs constitute ethical principles for living a meaningful and purposeful life; serving as a prescription for moral and ethical conduct and self-discipline. These principles direct attention towards one's health while acknowledging the spiritual aspects of one's nature. These eight limbs may be used separately, but within Yoga philosophy the physical postures and breathing exercises prepare the mind and body for meditation and spiritual development. Patanjali's eight limbs have given birth to many different yogic disciplines. Each has its own technique for preventing and treating disease. The most common aspects of yoga practice are the physical postures and breathing practices of **Hatha Yoga** and **Meditation**. Hatha Yoga enhances the capacity of the physical body through the use of a series of body postures, movements (asanas), and breathing techniques. The breathing techniques or **Pranayama** of Hatha Yoga focus on conscious prolongation of inhalation, breathe retention, and exhalation. It is through the unification of the physical body, breath, and concentration, while performing the postures and moments clean the blockages in the energy channels of the body.

Yoga is accepted as a form of mind-body medicine that integrates an individual's physical, mental and spiritual components to improve aspects of health, particularly stress-related illnesses. Yoga encourages one to relax, slow the breath and focus on the present, shifting the balance from the sympathetic nervous system and the flight-or-fight response to the parasympathetic system and the relaxation response. The latter is calming and restorative; it lowers breathing, and heart rate, decreases blood pressure, lowers cortisol levels, and increases blood flow to the intestines and vital organs. Mental health problems such as depression, anxiety, stress, and insomnia are among the most common reasons for individuals to seek treatment with complementary therapies such as yoga. One of the main objectives of yoga is to achieve tranquillity of mind and create a sense of well-being, feeling of relaxation, improved self-confidence and efficiency, increased attentiveness, lowered irritability and an optimistic outlook on life. The practice of yoga generates balanced energy which is vital to the function of the immune system. Yoga leads to an inhibition of the posterior or sympathetic area of the hypothalamus. This inhibition optimizes the body's sympathetic responses to stressful stimuli and restores autonomic regulatory reflex mechanisms associated with stress. Yogic practices inhibit the areas responsible for fear, aggressiveness and rage, and stimulate the rewarding pleasure centres in the medial forebrain and other areas leading to a state of bliss and pleasure. This inhibition results in lower anxiety, heart rate, respiratory rate, blood pressure and cardiac output. Evidence shows that stress contributes to the aetiology of heart disease, cancer and stroke as well as other chronic conditions and diseases. Since stress gives rise to numerous diseases, it is important to focus on stress management and reduction of negative emotional states. Yoga can be perceived as a holistic stress management technique that produces a physiological sequence of events in the body reducing the stress response. The scientific study of yoga has increased considerably in recent years and many clinical trials have been designed to assess its therapeutic effects and benefits. **Therapeutic yoga** is defined as the application of yoga postures and practices for the treatment of health conditions. Yoga therapy involves instruction in yogic practices and teachings to prevent, reduce, or relieve structural, physiological, emotional and spiritual pain and sufferings. Yogic practices enhance muscular strength and body flexibility, promote and improve respiratory and cardiovascular function. Yoga helps to rectify drug-seeking behaviours, reduce stress, anxiety, depression, improve sleep patterns, and enhance overall well-being and quality of life. Now-a-days a range of therapeutic approaches is available for the management of depressive disorders. However, patients turn to complementary therapies due to various adverse effects of medication and sometimes due to out of these medications, lack of response. A number of studies demonstrate the potential positive effects of Yoga interventions on depression, stress, and anxiety. Enhanced flexibility is one of the first and most obvious benefits of yoga. With continued practice comes a gradual loosening of the muscles and connective tissues surrounding the bones and joints that results in reduced aches and pains. Yoga helps build muscle mass and maintain muscle strength, which protects from conditions such as arthritis, osteoporosis and back pain. Yoga increases blood flow and levels of haemoglobin and red blood cells which allows for more oxygen to reach the body cells enhancing their function. Yoga also thins the blood which can decrease the risk of heart attack and stroke as they are often caused by blood clots. Though Yoga is not a cure for cancer, nor it can be taken as prevention, it increases physical, emotional and spiritual wellness. Yoga, breathing exercises, and meditation can reduce stress, promote healing, and enhance quality of life for patients with cancer. While practicing yoga, one is conscious of accepting moment-to-moment experiences creating mindfulness without depriving the body of its comfort zone. It is a well-known fact that stress has a negative impact on the immune system. Prolonged exposure to stress increases susceptibility to disease and mental health problems such as anxiety and depression. Tension is released through body postures, energy flows more readily throughout the body and allows to experience a sense of increased well-being and strength as well as a balance of mind, body, and spirit. Hence, practicing yoga and meditation as a means to manage and relieve both acute and chronic stress helps individuals overcome other co-morbidities associated with diseases and helps leading a healthy life. Through the process of meditation, when we direct our attention within, we are able to tap into the perennial source of permanent peace, bliss, and joy. Yoga's ability to increase relaxation and inducing a balanced mental state was studied to evaluate its effect on sleep quality and improving insomnia. It was found that Yoga has a positive influence on sleep patterns. Yoga and meditation practices have a positive influence on addictive behaviours. Through the practice of Yoga, addicts shift from self-inflicted harm and disrespect toward their bodies to more respectful, caring, and loving behaviours. Researchers are keen to understand how disciplines such as yoga promote personal growth, health, and well-being. By acknowledging the unity of mind, body and spirit, **mind-body fitness programs** can assist people in their calling for peace, calmness, and greater wholeness and integration in their lives. Health care professionals need to be aware of the potential of Yoga as an important component of a personal wellness plan. Yoga should be practiced with wisdom and modified to meet individual needs and goals. The length of the induction phase varies depending on an individual's initial level of fitness and health status. While modern medicine has the ability in many cases to heal physical diseases and alleviate psychological disorders, it is argued that a purely medical approach is far less effective in healing emotional, intellectual, and personality layers of the human entity. The discipline of yoga offers individuals a timeless and holistic model of health and healing. It may not result in the complete elimination of physical diseases; however, it offers a holistic path of healing. There exists a connection between a person's overall physical and mental health and the inner peace and well-being. Yoga is designed to strengthen this connection. It is a science; science of well-being and youthfulness, for integrating body, mind, and soul. When we do yoga, deep breathing, stretching, moments that release muscle tension, relaxed focus on being present in the body, we initiate a process that turns the fight-or-flight system off and the relaxation response on. It has a miraculous effect on the body. The heartbeat slows respiration and blood pressure decrease. Yoga encourages us to focus on our breathing and the sensations in our body. Yoga does not take time; it gives time in the true sense of the term. The reward of doing yoga is simple. We can be at peace with ourselves while living a fulfilling life.

Yoga encompasses eight life principles:

- Yama (moral code)
- Niyama (Self-discipline)
- Asana (Postures or Poses)
- Pranayama (Mindfulness of breathing)
- Pratyahara (Detachment from senses)
- Dharana (concentration)
- Dhyana (Meditation or mindful focus on the present)
- Samadhi (Ecstasy)

It is to be noted that the asanas are focused on physical experiences. The others concern mental, emotional, and spiritual experiences. This is because yoga is much more focused on the practitioner's inner experiences than their outer experiences. An authentic yoga practice demands introspection, reflection, and intense consideration of the self. It is a way to connect with our own thoughts, feelings, beliefs, and core values, opening the window into our deeper selves. True, Yoga and psychology are interdependent; however, yoga is intimately related to the subfields of positive psychology. The link between yoga and positive psychology is a strong one. Although Yoga started with a slightly different focus, it is now commonly practiced as an attempt to enhance well-being. Well-being is a central topic in positive psychology, which explains the frequent use of yoga in intervention and exercises. Further, Yoga offers an excellent opportunity to enter into flow, the state of being fully engaged and present in the moment. Practicing yoga can help people cultivate mindfulness, develop greater awareness, and improve their ability to focus on what is at hand. Yoga teaches us to cure what need not be endured and endure what cannot be cured. It is a science; science of well-being, youthfulness and integrating body, mind, and soul. It does not just change the way we see things, it transforms the person who sees. The ultimate purpose of Yoga is to always observe things accurately, and, therefore, never act in a way that will make us regret our actions later.

Physical Benefits of Yoga

Although Yoga may seem like a relatively mild form of exercise, regular Yoga practice can result in the same health benefits as many other types of exercise. Yoga is even more beneficial than most types of exercises. People who practice Yoga regularly are more likely to report higher energy, better moods, greater happiness, more fulfilling relationships with others, and more satisfying lives in general. Yoga is able to decrease levels of cortisol, a stress hormone that influences **levels of serotonin,** the neurotransmitter often associated with **depression**. Practicing Yoga can help improve breathing and lung function. Yoga can be helpful to reduce migraine frequency which is severe recurring headaches. It encourages mindfulness, which may be used to help promote mindful and healthy eating habits. In addition to improving flexibility, Yoga is a great addition to an exercise routine for its strength-building benefits. These benefits include

- Give more energy.
- Boosts metabolism.
- Improves skin condition.
- Strengthens the joints.
- Lubricates and strengthens spine.
- Improves body posture.
- Adds strength and beauty to body, mind, and soul.
- Reduces fatigue.
- Enhances flexibility.
- Helps maintain a healthy heart rate.
- Improves kidney function.
- Reduces obesity.
- Helps sleep better.
- Inhibits inflammation in the body.

Physical activities to enhance positivity
- Practical relaxation / meditation
- Have proper diet and take adequate sleep
- Walking / Jogging
- Skipping or cycling
- Playing badminton
- Gardening

Social Dimension of Yoga

The social dimension of Yoga improves social and occupational functioning and improves quality of life. Primary socialization, which is the most important aspect of personality development, takes place during childhood, usually within the family. By responding to the approval and disapproval of parents and other elder members of the family, the child learns the language and many of the basic behaviour patterns. The process of socialization is not confined to childhood, but continues throughout life and teaches the growing child about the norms and regulations of the society. Some key elements of this process include respect for others, listening carefully to other persons, being interested in them and speaking out our thoughts and feelings politely with a sense of acceptance and being non-judgemental. It implies that instead of focusing on what we should have been feeling or experiencing, we get aware of our real feeling. It is not about trying to change anything; we just monitor our experience at the moment. **Mindfulness Based Stress Reduction (MBSR)** program has its roots in Buddhist Meditation. A long body of research has established mindfulness meditation as one of the most powerful and effective tools to promote psychological well-being. According to American Psychological Association, the research on mindfulness has identified the following benefits:

- Reduced rumination.
- Stress reduction.
- Increases in working memory.
- Increased ability to focus.
- Less emotional reactivity.
- More cognitive flexibility.
- Relationship satisfaction.

In the path of self-control, will power is the key. Yoga teaches us to cure what need not be endured and endure what cannot be cured. Yoga allows us to find an inner peace that is not disturbed by the endless stresses and struggles of life. It is beneficial to practice the following for inner peace and tranquillity:

- Practice daily prayer.
- Meet your friends, share your thoughts.
- Inculcate support for yourself with your family/ neighbour.

Emotional Dimension of Yoga

Positive psychology is secular in all aspects. It gives equal importance to quantitative analyses like depression and happiness scales, and at the same time also embraces qualitative and self-enhancing practices like Yoga, meditation, and mindfulness. Any yoga practice, be that flow meditation or other popular methods, provides relaxing feeling to mind and body. Practicing yoga can help people cultivate mindfulness, develop greater awareness, and improve their ability to focus on what is at hand. The benefits of yoga on emotional dimension may be comprised of the following aspects.

- Builds confidence.
- Helps us learn to breathe, both literally and metaphorically.
- Makes us more mindful.
- Boosts us strength and endurance.
- Helps relieve stress.

To get the greater benefits of Yoga, begin the day with the following beliefs.

- I am a peaceful and loving soul. I will remain peaceful throughout the day.
- For the entire day, I will remain cool whatever may come on my way.
- Problems are normal in life. These are platforms to examine my strengths and resilience.
- Inherent in any problem there is a solution. I will try to find out the solution without losing my hope and patience.

Yoga is effective in lessening symptoms of depression reducing fatigue, relieving anxiety, reducing stress, and often boosts feelings of self-confidence and self-esteem. It can be especially helpful for those struggling with Post-Traumatic Stress Disorder (PTSD). The results of yoga on PTSD symptoms highlight this link between the body and the brain, and the potential of yoga to facilitate this connection. Many PTSD symptoms are physical, such as increased heart rate and perspiration that sometimes are accompanied by vivid memories of the trauma. Yoga may be especially helpful in addressing such symptoms it can concentrate on the physical symptoms of stress, anxiety, fear, and depression. There is a growing amount of research on the correlation between practicing meditation and undoing negative bias from the mind. Research has found that meditation may help people become more conscious of their own prejudices. It is found that just ten minutes of mindfulness meditation reduced the automatic activation of negative associations. A daily meditation practice trains us to notice our thoughts and become more self-conscious. It implies that this can reduce amygdala reactivity overtime. Hence, we are less likely to be affected by immediate reactions and fear response generated by amygdala. Moreover, meditation is about treating ourselves and others with compassion and without judgement. Mindfulness makes us to be non-judgemental, and detach ourselves from a strong negative pathway of thought. When we practice genuine meditation, we can condition our brain to react more compassionately. Moreover, intellectual development is related to the development of our mental abilities and processes such as critical thinking, memory, perception, decision making, imagination, creativity, etc. Development of this cognitive dimension is very important as it enables us to learn new things and acquire knowledge and skills. Yogic practices such as asana, pranayama, dhyana (meditation) help to develop concentration, memory, and thereby help in intellectual development. Stress and burnout is an integral part of our life. Stress management exercises and assessments promote the overall physical and mental well-being. However, positive psychology is not a resort to fight distress or disappointments with the help of yoga. With practice of yoga, we become aware of how and where we are restricted, in body, mind, and heart; and how gradually to overcome restrictions. When these mental restraints are cleared, we feel free and energetic. We become more harmonious and at ease with ourselves. Our lives begin to flow. Yoga is a way of moving into stillness in order to experience the truth of **who you are**. Hence, the body benefits from movement, and the mind benefits from stillness. It is the journey of the self, thorough the self, to the self.

A beautiful positive psychology intervention that we can follow as a daily practice and imbibe into our personality is the **art of forgiving**. When we hold on to grudges and complaints against others, it destroys our inner peace and prosperity. Take a piece of paper and name all the people and the incidents of the past that hurt you. Besides each name, describe how the negative encounter had hurt you. Try to name all the feeling you experienced in that phase (sad, angry, insulted, hopeless, heartbroken, betrayed, hateful, and the like).

- While you are writing about all the negative encounters, notice how those depressing feelings start coming back to you.
- Now close your eyes take two deep breaths and relax for a few seconds.
- Next, imagine each name on the list and in your heart; say 'I **forgive you**'. Alternatively, if you were at fault, admit it and ask for their forgiveness.
- Notice how this exchange of forgiveness liberates you from the pent up grudges and make you feel empowered from the core.
- Open your eyes and on the paper where you had listed the grievances, write in bolds, **Forgiven and Free**.

Spiritual Dimension of Yoga

This dimension is related to the development of values. It is also concerned with self-actualization which is related to recognizing one's potential and developing them to the maximum. Proper development of this dimension helps the person to realize his true identity. For spiritual development, Yama, Niyama, Pratyahara, and Dhyana (Meditation) are helpful. Yama and Niyama help to develop our moral values while pranayama and meditation help us to realize our true self. Introspection is very effective for the development of **self**. Yama (Restraint) and Niyama (Observance) are principles which need to be adopted always in our day-to-day life. Principles of Yama are concerned with one's social life; while the principles of Niyama are concerned with one's personal life. Yama and Niyama are part of Ashtanga Yoga. The five principles of Yama are:

- Ahimsa (Non-violence)
- Satya (truthfulness)
- Asteya (Non-Stealing)
- Brahmcharya (Abstinence)
- Aparigraha (Non-collectiveness)

The principles of Niyama are:

- Shaucha (Cleanliness)
- Santosha (Satisfaction)
- Tapas (Austerity)

For experiencing inner peace and compassion, sit comfortably and relax. Now focus your attention on your breathing. Let it find its own calm rhythm gently breathe in peacefulness and breathe out any negative feelings. Allow your mind to slow down do not judge your thoughts as good or bad, accept them as it is and let them go.

- Now focus on your inner peace; that place, that is deep within yourself; that is peaceful; where your inner compassion (kindness) and forgiveness lies. Here you are patient, tolerant, generous and understanding. All these qualities are here which make up your inner compassion. Experience the feeling of compassion and see it is focused on a point; a point of light situated at the centre of your forehead.

- Now raise your awareness beyond yourself to a place of unlimited peace; see it first as a small point of light. As you move towards it, it becomes brighter. It is like an ocean of peace a space of calm, love, and compassion. You feel connected to that ocean of deep peace and love. It surrounds you like a shawl; it fills you up, absorbing every part of you with comfortable warmth.
- Rest in that feeling of being loved. It is like energy, vibration or light filling you until you overflow.
- Now slowly you move away from the ocean as a point of light. You will have the memory of being loved and can reconnect at any time you want.
- Gradually become aware of your body.

Spiritual dimension is the Bhakti Yoga, the path of surrender. It diminishes our identity and gives us knowledge and peace. Bhakti Yoga takes away fear anxiety and worry and keeps us peaceful. We feel blissful and happy with the help of Yoga.

Questions

Chapter 1 History of Positive Psychology

Short Questions

- What are the three waves of psychology prior to positive psychology?
- What do you understand by the Disease Model of Psychology?
- Who are the pioneers of Behaviourism?
- Who developed classical conditioning?
- What is Behaviourism?
- What is behaviourism according to Skinner?
- What is the third wave in psychology?
- What is humanistic psychology?
- Define existential anxiety.
- What is positive psychology?
- Which tradition is the core root of positive psychology?
- Define eudaimonia.
- What are hedonic approaches to good life?
- What is eudaimonic approaches to good life?
- Define good life as viewed by positive psychology.
- Define pleasant life.
- What is the other name of meaningful life?
- What are the goals of positive psychology?

Long Questions

- What is positive psychology? Discuss in detail the three waves in psychology prior to positive psychology.
- What are the three overlapping areas of research in positive psychology? Discuss the goals of positive psychology in this context.

- Discuss in detail the history of positive psychology.
- "Aristotelian tradition is the core root of positive psychology", elucidate the statement.

Chapter 2 Pioneers of Positive Psychology

Short Questions

- Define humanistic psychology
- Explain Maslow's hierarchy of needs.
- Define meta-motivation according to Maslow.
- Define Maslow's Deficiency Cognition.
- What is self-efficacy according to Bandura?
- Which came first - social cognitive theory or social learning theory?
- Are self-efficacy and motivation related? If yes, give the explanations.
- How self-efficacy and resilience are related?
- How self-efficacy is different from self-confidence?
- Explain locus of control.
- Are self-efficacy and locus of control related?
- Self-efficacy and stress are related. Explain how?
- Explain social cognitive theory of Bandura.
- What are the six constructs of social cognitive theory of Bandura?
- Define self-concept.
- How can we improve self-efficacy?
- Why Carol Dweck is famous in the field of psychology?
- What is fixed mind-set according to Dweck.
- Define growth mind-set.

Long Questions

- Discuss Maslow's contribution to humanistic psychology with special reference to Maslow's hierarchy of needs.
- What is self-efficacy? Elucidate Bandura's self-efficacy theory.
- Can self-efficacy be improved? Elucidate.
- Explain in detail Carol Dweck's contribution to the field of psychology with special reference to mind set.

• Explain in detail social cognitive theory of Bandura.

Chapter 3 Contribution of Martin Seligman to Positive Psychology

Short Questions

• What are the broad areas of research of Martin Seligman?
• What was the mission of positive psychology centre at the University of Pennsylvania?
• What is learned helplessness?
• What is the idea behind the theory of learned helplessness?
• How learned helplessness leads to clinical depression?
• What are the four levels of analysis for positive psychology?
• What are the two major wellsprings of interest for positive psychology?
• Explain the process of interest for positive psychology.
• Define the mechanisms of interest to positive psychology.
• What are the outcomes of interest of positive psychology?
• Who developed PERMA?
• What are the five facts of well-being for PERMA?
• What is flourishing?
• How many classes of virtues are described in Seligman's character strengths and virtues Manual?
• What is the number of character strengths that comprise the six virtues?
• Define Aristotelian Model of virtues.
• What is the difference between strengths and talents?
• What are the main criteria for character strength of each trait?
• Define character strengths.
• Name the six classes of virtues as recommended by Seligman.
• Name the ten principles of character strengths.
• Define Signature Strengths.

Long Questions

- Define positive psychology. Elucidate Seligman's four levels of analysis for positive psychology.
- Discuss in detail Seligman's PERMA Model as an influential model in positive psychology.
- Discuss in detail Seligman's work on character strengths and virtues in positive psychology.
- Discuss in detail the principles of character strengths as given by Seligman.
- What is flourishing? Explain how Seligman distinguished between four levels of analysis for positive psychology.

Chapter 4 Positive Emotions

Short Questions

- Define emotion.
- Who developed Broaden-and-Build theory?
- What are the most commonly experienced positive emotions according to Fredrickson?
- Explain Broaden-and-Build theory of Fredrickson.
- What are the health benefits of positive emotions?
- Do positive emotions facilitate psychological well-being?
- Explain positive social engagement.
- How positive emotions foster resilience and memory?
- Write ten words to reflect positive emotion.

Long Questions

- What is the role of positive emotions in maintaining positivity? Discuss Broaden-and-Build theory of Fredrickson in this context.
- What is Broaden-and-Build theory of Fredrickson? Discuss its application and importance in the work place.
- Elucidate Broaden-and-Build theory with reference to its health benefits.

+ "Positive emotions facilitate psychological well-being". Justify the statement.

+ Justify the statement that positive emotions foster resilience and memory.

Chapter 5 Positive Individual Traits and Positive Subjective Experiences

Short Questions

+ What is creativity?
+ What are the five stages of creativity?
+ What is convergent thinking?
+ What is divergent thinking?
+ What are the three major characteristics of creative personality?
+ What is curiosity?
+ What are the three types of courage?
+ What is compassion?
+ What is the role of compassion in well-being?
+ Define self-control.
+ What is the role of self-control in health and well-being?
+ Explain integrity.
+ What is the role of integrity in improving quality of life.
+ Define positive subjective experiences?
+ Explain the role of positive subjective experiences in positive psychology?
+ What is peak-end-theory of Kahneman?
+ What is the 'experiencing self' according to Kahneman?
+ Explain the 'narrating self' as said by Kahneman.
+ What is Eureka moment?
+ What is mere exposure effect?
+ Explain endowment effect.
+ What is adaptation?

Long Questions

- Discuss in detail any three major positive traits of the individual.
- What is creativity? Discuss Wallas Stage Model of Creativity.
- Explain Guilford's views on creativity with special reference to characteristics of creative personality.
- What is peak-end-theory of Kahneman? Explain it in the context of positive subjective experiences.

Chapter 6 Flow and Happiness

Short Questions

- What is flow?
- What is metaphor of flow?
- What are the other names used for metaphor of flow?
- What is vital engagement?
- What are the five major components of flow?
- Explain Autotelic experience.
- What are the conditions of flow?
- Who experiences flow?
- What are the mechanisms of flow?
- State any two major positive consequences of flow.
- What are the negative consequences of flow?
- What is happiness?
- Explain hedonic approach to happiness?
- What is subjective well-being?
- What is Eudaimonia according to Aristotle?
- Explain Eudaimonic well-being?
- Explain Eudaimonic happiness.
- Explain self-determination theory.
- State any five major sources of happiness.
- What is savouring?
- What is set-point theory of happiness?
- What is life satisfaction theory of happiness?

- How the emotional state view departs from hedonism?
- What are the three broad categories of affective states that are involved in happiness?
- What are the two basic concepts behind Eudaimonic theory of happiness?

Long Questions

- What is flow? Elucidate the components of flow.
- Who experiences flow? Discuss the mechanisms of flow.
- Critically examine the consequences of flow.
- Elucidate the meaning and nature of happiness.
- What is happiness? Discuss the sources of happiness with special reference to savouring.
- Critically examine the two major theories of happiness.
- What is set point theory of happiness? Do personality profiles affect happiness? Explain.
- Elucidate Life Satisfaction and Affective State theories of happiness.

Chapter 7 Altruism, Hope, and Optimism

Short Questions

- What is altruism?
- What is altruistic behaviour?
- What causes people to be altruistic?
- Is altruism a part of human nature?
- Is altruism learned or innate?
- Is altruism dependent upon happiness of the individual?
- What is nepotistic altruism?
- What is reciprocal altruism?
- Do social norms influence altruism?
- What are the cognitive reasons of altruism?
- What is Empathy-Altruism hypothesis?
- What is Negative-State Relief Model?
- What is hope?

- Is hope positive or negative?
- What are the two separate components of goal-directed expectations according to Snyder's view?
- What is agency according to Snyder?
- What are Snyder's views on pathways?
- What exactly is optimism?
- What is the difference between optimism and hope?
- What is the Latin word from which optimism is derived from?
- What is dispositional optimism?
- What are the attributes linked to optimism?
- What is Little optimism?
- What is Big optimism?
- What are the qualities generated by positive attitude?
- What is positive illusion?
- What is Learned optimism?
- State any three of the major means to increase optimism.
- What are the health benefits of optimism?

Long Questions
- What is altruism? Discuss the various forms of altruism.
- What is hope? Elucidate the components of hope.
- What is optimism? Discuss the relationship between optimism and emotional well-being.
- Can optimism be increased? Discuss the means of enhancing optimism.
- What is optimism? Discuss the benefits of optimism.

Chapter 8 Positive Thinking and Resilience

Short Questions
- What is positive thinking?
- What is optimistic explanatory style?
- What is pessimistic explanatory style?
- What are the health benefits of positive thinking?

- How do you train your mind to think positive?
- Why positive thinking is important?
- What is positive affirmation?
- What is an example of positive affirmation?
- What is positive reappraisal?
- What is resilience?
- What personality factors help in enhancing resilience?
- What factors within the family contribute to resilience?
- What factors within the community contribute to resilience?
- How self-acceptance is helpful in developing resilience in adult life?
- What is personal growth?
- What is environmental mastery?

Long Questions

- What is positive thinking? Discuss the ways how positive thinking can be improved?
- Discuss the health benefits of positive thinking?
- What is resilience? What are the factors helpful in enhancing resilience in childhood?
- Elucidate the factors helpful in enhancing resilience in adulthood.

Chapter 9 Emotional Intelligence

Short Questions

- What is Emotional Intelligence?
- Who popularized the concept of Emotional Intelligence?
- Who described Emotional Intelligence as Social Intelligence?
- What are the four different levels of Emotional Intelligence?
- Name the five emotional competencies as suggested by Goleman.
- State the five components of Emotional Intelligence.
- What are the four domains of Emotional Intelligence according to Goleman.
- What are the three dominant characteristics of Emotional Intelligence according to Block?

- Define Emotional Quotient (EQ).
- Which section of the brain is involved in emotional intelligence?
- Which section helps coordinate responses that trigger an emotional response?
- Is emotional intelligence important?
- What are the benefits of emotional intelligence at work place?
- How emotional intelligence is helpful in leadership behaviour?
- Are Intelligence (IQ) and Emotional Intelligence (EQ) opposing competencies?

Long Questions

- What is Emotional Intelligence (EQ)? Discuss the levels and components of emotional intelligence.
- Define Emotional Intelligence EQ. Elaborate Goleman's four domains of intelligence.
- Discuss the importance of emotional intelligence at work place.
- Discuss the role of emotional intelligence in effective leadership.
- Elucidate the importance of emotional intelligence for the benefits of the organization.

Chapter 10 Stress and its Management

Short Questions

- What is stress according to WHO?
- Which is considered as one of the earliest models of stress?
- Which chemical is released when we are under stress?
- What are the physical symptoms of stress?
- What are the emotional symptoms of stress?
- State the cognitive symptoms of stress.
- State the behavioural symptoms of stress.
- What is a stressor?
- Define external stressors.
- Name any five of the major internal stressors?
- What are the effects of chronic stress?

- What is Diathesis-Stress Model?
- What are the two contributing factors necessary to cause disease?
- Name any five illnesses induced by stress.
- What is Post Traumatic Stress Disorder (PTSD)?
- Define coping behaviour.
- What are the goals of coping?
- What are the two basic styles of coping?
- How do you explain coping strategies?
- Distinguish between problem-focused and emotion-focused coping strategy.
- What are the factors that influence coping strategies?
- What is social coping?
- What is meaning-focused coping?
- What is proactive coping?
- Define locus of control.
- Distinguish between Internals and Externals.
- What is Myers-Briggs Type Indicator (MBTI).
- What are the five basic dimensions of personality according to MBTI?
- What are the characteristics of Type-A behaviour?
- Define optimism.
- How optimism is related to coping strategies?
- What is mastery?
- How personal hardiness and resilience are correlated?
- What are the different types of social support?
- What is Progressive Muscle Relaxation (PMR)?
- What is cognitive restructuring?
- What is emotional expression?

Long Questions

- Define stress. Discuss the signs and symptoms of stress.
- What is 'flight or fight' model of Cannon? Discuss the various causes of stress.

- What is Diathesis- Stress Model? Discuss various stress related diseases.
- What is coping with stress? Elucidate the various types of coping strategies.
- Discuss the personality factors contributing to coping mechanisms.
- Define social support. Elucidate the role of social support in coping with stress.
- Discuss in detail the various stress management strategies.

Chapter 11 Mental Health and Psychological Well-Being

Short Questions

- Define mental health.
- Which day of the year is celebrated as the World Mental Health Day?
- What is identity crisis?
- State at least any five symptoms of major depressive disorder.
- Explain Biopsychosocial approach to mental health issues.
- What are the major psychological factors related to mental health problems?
- State the social factors responsible for mental health problems.
- What are the two perspectives of prevention and intervention strategies of mental health?
- How to reduce health-compromising behaviours?
- What are the important factors to increase health-enhancing behaviour?
- State five major tips for nurturing good mental health.
- Define well-being.
- What are the different aspects of well-being?
- What are the factors that facilitate emotional well-being?
- What are the major facilitators of physical well-being?
- What are the factors contributing to social well-being?

- What is workplace well-being?
- What is societal well-being?
- What are the major components of societal well-being?
- Define subjective well-being.
- What is cognitive appraisal?
- What is affective appraisal?
- What is psychological well-being?
- Who developed psychological well-being theory?
- What are the factors associated with psychological well-being?
- What are the components of psychological well-being?
- What is self-acceptance?
- State the importance of social interaction.
- What is personal growth?

Long Questions

- Define mental health. Discuss the issues and challenges of mental health.
- Elucidate various approaches to mental health issues.
- What is mental health? Discuss the prevention and intervention strategies for nurturing good mental health.
- Discuss various tips for enjoying good mental health.
- Discuss in detail different aspects of well-being.
- What is psychological well-being? Discuss the components of psychological well-being.
- Discuss psychological well-being with reference to various factors associated with it.

Chapter 12 Ways to Positive Psychology

Short Questions

- How positive psychology is useful to the counselling field?
- What is Ellis Rational – Emotive Behavioural therapy?
- What are the different ways to improve well-being of people?
- What is the goal of Positive Psychology Interventions (PPIs)?

- What is meant by savouring PPIs?
- What is meaning oriented PPI?
- State any five major factors of happiness according to Fordyce.

Long Questions

- Elucidate the statement, "Positive Psychology is useful to the counselling field in many ways".
- Explain the various empirically supported ways to improve well-being of people.
- Explain gratitude. How it is helpful in enhancing self-contentment and joy? Elucidate.
- Explain mindfulness. State its importance to handle obstacles to help us live our best lives.
- Elucidate the role of Positive Psychology Interventions (PPIs) in building and broadening the lives of individuals.

Chapter 13 Helping Positivity

Short Questions

- Define Yoga.
- What is Ashtanga Yoga?
- What is therapeutic Yoga?
- What is Yoga therapy?
- What are the benefits of Yoga?
- What are the life principles of Yoga?
- What are the strength- building benefits of Yoga?
- What are the benefits of mindfulness?
- What are the physical activities helpful for enhancing positivity?
- What are the social dimensions of Yoga?
- What are the benefits of Yoga on emotional dimension?
- What are the symptoms of Post Traumatic Stress Disorder (PTSD)?
- What are the five principles of Yama?
- State the principles of Niyama.

Long Questions

- Define Yoga. Discuss its importance in our day-to-day life.
- What are the principles of Yoga? Discuss the physical benefits of Yoga.
- Explain Yoga and its emotional dimension.
- Explain Yoga and its social dimension.
- Explain Yoga and its spiritual dimension.

References

Algoe, S.B., Gable, S.L., & Maisel, N.C.(2010). It's the little things: Everyday gratitude as a booster shot for romantic relationship. *Personal Relationships*, 17(2), 217-233.

Aristotle (2000). *Nicomachean Ethics*, Trans. R. Crisp. Cambridge: Cambridge University Press.

Aspinwall, L.G., & Taylor, S.E. (1997). A stitch in time: Self-regulation and proactive coping. *Psychological Bulletin, 121(3)*, 417-436.

Atkin, L.B., Dunn, E.W., Whillans, A.V., Grant, A.M., and Norton, M.I. (2013). Making a difference matters: Impact unlocks the emotional benefits of prosocial spending. *Journal of Economic Behaviour Organization*, 88, 90-95.

Bandura, A. (1965). Behavioural modification through modelling procedures. In L. Krasner and L.P. Ullman (Eds.), Research in behaviour modification, 310-340, New York: Holt.

Bandura, A. (1973). *Aggression: A social learning analysis*. Prentice- Hall.

Bandura, A. (1988). The explanatory and predictive scope of self-efficacy theory. *Journal of Clinical and Social Psychology, 4*, 350-373.

Baum, A. (1990). Stress, intrusive imagery, and chronic distress. *Health Psychology, 9*, 653-675.

Blanchard, G.T. (2013). *Transcending trauma: Post-traumatic growth following physical, sexual, and emotional abuse.* Brandon, VT: Safer Society Press.

Brickman, P., & Campell, D.T. (1971). Hedonic relativism and planning the good society. In M.H. Appley (Ed.), *Adaptation-level theory*, New York: Academic.

Bryant, F., Veroff, J. (2007). *Savouring: A new model of positive experience.* Mahwah, NJ: Lawrence Erlbaum Associates, Inc.

Buck, B. et al. (2008). Positive Psychology and Student Engagement. *Journal of Cross Disciplinary Perspectives in Education, (No. 1)*, 28-35.

Buckworth, J. Dishman, R.K. (2002). *Exercise Psychology*: United Sates: Human Kinetics.

Buss, D.M. (1991). *Learned Optimism: How to change your mind and your life.*

Byrne, P. (2000). Stigma of Mental Illness and Ways of Diminishing it. *Advances in Psychiatric Treatment*, 6, 65-72.

Calhoun, L.G., & Tedeschi, R.G.(2012). *Post-traumatic growth in clinical practice.* New York, NY: Routledge.

Cannon, W.B. (1932). *The Wisdom of the body.* New York: Norton.

Carstensen, I.V. et al. (1999). Taking time seriously: A theory of socio-emotional selectivity. *American Psychologists, 54*, 165-181.

Carver, C.S. (1998). Resilience and thriving: Issues, models, and linkages. *Journal of social Issues, 54*, 245-266.

Carver, C.S., &Scheier, M.F. (1990). Origins and functions of positive and negative affect: A control-process view. In Peterson, C. (2006). *A primer in positive psychology.* New York: Oxford University Press.

Carver, C.S., &Scheier, M.F. (2002). *Psychological Inquiry, 13(4)* 288-290.

Chandola, T. et al. (2008). Work stress and coronary heart disease: what are the mechanisms? *European Heart Journal, 29*.640-648.

Chou, C. et al., (2013). Positive Psychology, Theory, Research, and Practice: A primer for Rehabilitation. *Counselling Professionals*, Rehabilitation Research, Policy, and Education, *27(3)*, 131-153.

Cohen, F., & Lazarus, R. (1979). Coping with the stresses of illness. In G.C. Stone, F. Cohen, & N. E. Adler (Eds.), *Health Psychology: A handbook, I,* 217-254, San Francisco: Jossey-Bass.

Crompton, W.C. (2005). An Introduction to Positive Psychology, Belmont, California, Wadsworth Publishing.

Csikszentmihalyi, M. (1990). *Flow: The Psychology of Optimal Experience.* New York: Harper Row.

Csikszentmihalyi, M. (1991). *Flow the psychology of optimal experience: steps towards enhancing the quality of life.* New York: Harper Collins.

Csikszentmihalyi, M. (2002). Flow: *The classic work on how to achieve happiness.* London: Rider.

Deci, E.L., Ryan, R.M. (2008). Hedonia, eudaimonia, and well-being. An introduction. *Journal of Happiness Studies, 9,* 1-11.

Dianne, H. (2010). *An invitation to Health, Brief.* Psychological Well-being, 2010-2011 edition. Wadsworth Language learning.

Diener, E. (2000). Subjective well-being. The science of happiness and a proposal for a national index. *American Psychologist, 55,* 34-43.

Duckworth, A.L., Steen, T.A., & Seligman, E.P. (2005). Positive Psychology in clinical practice. *Annual Review of Clinical Psychology, 1,* 629-651.

Dweck, C.S. (2006). *Mind-set: The New Psychology of Success.* New York: Random House.

Easterlin, R.A.(2005). Building a better theory of well-being in L. Bruni and Porta eds. *Economics and Happiness: Framing the Analysis*: Oxford University Press.

Ellis, A. (2002) Rational Emotive Behaviour Therapy. *Encyclopaedia of Psychotherapy. Vol. 2*, 483-487.

Erikson, E. (1998). *Identity: and Crisis*. New York: Norton.

Etuk, E.S.(2006). Recipe for success. The 21 indispensable things that can help you succeed in life. *Emida International Publishers*. New Delhi.

Fava, G., & Ruini, C. (2003). Development and characteristics of a well-being enhancing psychotherapeutic strategy: well-being therapy. *Journal of Behaviour Therapy and Experimental Psychiatry, 34(1)*, 45-63.

Folkman, S., Schaefer, C., & Lazarus, R.S. (1979). Cognitive processes as mediators of stress and coping. In V. Hamilton & D.M. Warburton (Eds.), *Human stress and cognition: An information-processing approach*, Wiley, London, 265 – 298.

Fordyce, M.W. (1983). A program to increase happiness: Further Studies. *Journal of Counselling Psychology, 30(4)*, 483-498.

Fredrickson, B.L. (1998). *Psychological Inquiry, 9 (4)*, 279 – 281.

Fredrickson, B.L. (2000). *Cultivating Positive emotions to optimize health and well-being. Prevention and treatment, 3(1)*, Article 1.

Fredrickson, B.L.(2001). The role of positive emotions in positive psychology. The broaden-and-build theory of positive emotions. *American Psychologist,56(3)*, 218-226.

Fredrickson, B.L. (2002). Positive emotions. In C.R. Snyder & S. Lopez (Eds.), *Handbook of Positive Psychology*.

Fredrickson, B.L. (2003). Positive emotions and stress. *Journal of Personality and Social Psychology,84(2)*, 365-76.

Fredrickson, B.L. (2004). *Gratitude, like other Positive Emotions, Broadens and Builds.* In R.A. Emmons, & M.E. Mc Cullough (Eds.).

Fredrickson, B.L., Maynard KE, Helm MJ, Haney TL, et al., (2000). Hostility predicts magnitude and duration of blood pressure response to anger. *Journal of Behavioural Medicine, 23*: 229-243.

Friedman, M., & Rosenman, R.H. (1959). Association of specific overt behaviour pattern with blood and cardiovascular findings: blood cholesterol level, blood clotting time, incidence of arcus senilis. *Journal of the American medical science.*

Friedman, M., & Rosenman, R.H. (1976). Multivariate prediction of coronary heart disease during 8.5 year follow-up in the Western Collaborative Group Study. The *American Journal of Cardiology, 37(6)*, 903-910.

Fromm, E. (1956). *The Art of Loving An Enquiry into the Nature of Love.* New York: Harper & Brothers.

Fromm, E. (1973). *The Anatomy of Human Destructiveness.* New York. Holt, Rinehart and Winston.

Fung, H.H., Carstensen, I.I. & Lang, F.R.(2001). Age-related patterns in social networks among European-American and African-American: Implications for Socioemotional Selectivity across the life span. *International Journal of Aging and Human Development, 52*, 185-206.

Gable, S.L., &Haidt, J. (2005). What (and why) is positive psychology? *Review of General Psychology, 9*, 103-110.

Galassi, J.P. &Akos, P. (2007). Strengths-based school Counselling: Promoting student development and achievement. New York, NY: Routledge.

Goleman.(1995). *Emotional Intelligence.* New York: Bantam Books.

Goleman, D. (1998). *Working with emotional intelligence.* New York: Bantam Books.

Goleman, D. (2002). *Working with emotional intelligence,* New York: Bantam Books.

Guilford, J.P. (1950). Creativity. *American Psychologist, 5,* 444-454.

Gunthert, K. C., Cohen, L.H., &Armeli, S. (1999). *Journal of Personality and Social Psychology, 77(5),* 1087-1100.

Haidt, J. (2006). *The happiness hypothesis: Finding modern truth in ancient wisdom.* New York, NY: Perseus Books Group.

Haybron, D.M. (2001). *Philosophy and Phenomenological Research, 62(3),* 501-528.

Henry, D.L. (1999). Resilience in maltreated children: Implications for special needs adoption, *Child Welfare, 78(5),* 519-540.

Huppert, F.A. (2009). Psychological Well-being: Evidence regarding its causes and consequences. *Applied Psychology: Health and Well-being, 1,* 137-164.

Jackson, S.A. (1992). Athletes in flow: A qualitative investigation of flow states in elite figure skaters. *Journal of Applied Sport Psychology, 4(2),* 161-180.

Kahneman, D. et al. (1991). Anomalies: The Endowment Effect, Loss Aversion, and Status Quo Bias. *Journal of Economic Perspectives, 5(1),* 193 - 206.

Kahneman, D., Fredickson, B.L. (1993). *Psychological Science, 4 (6),* 401 – 405.

Kahneman, D. (1999). Objective happiness. In D. Kahnemann E. Diener, & N. Schwarz (Eds.), Well-being: *The foundations of hedonic psychology,* New York: Russell Sage.

Keyes, C.L.M. (2003). *Flourishing: Positive Psychology.*

Knafo, A, & Israel, S. (2012). Empathy, Prosocial behaviour, and other aspects of kindness. In M. Zentner & R.L. Shiner (Eds.), *Handbook of temperament.* 168-179. New York, NY: Guilford Press.

Kobasa, D.M., & Maddi, S.R. (1999). Early experiences in hardiness development. *Consulting Psychology Journal, 51,* 106-116.

Kress, V.E., & Paylo, M.J. (2014). *Treating those with mental disorders: A strength-based, comprehensive approach to case conceptualization and treatment.* Upper Saddle River, NJ: Merrill.

Layous, K., Nelsen, S.K., & Lyubomisky, S. (2013). What is the optimal way to deliver a positive activity intervention? The cause of writing about one's best possible selves. *Journal of Happiness Studies, 14(2),* 635-654.

Lazarus, R.S. (1993). From psychological stress to the emotions: A history of changing outlooks. *Annual Review of Psychology, 44:* 1-22.

Lazarus, R.S., & Folkman, S. (1984). *Stress, appraisal and coping.* New York: Springer.

Lehman, P., & Simmons, C.A., (2009). *Strengths-based better interventions: A new paradigm in ending family violence.* New York, NY: Springer.

Linley, P.A., et al., (2010). Using signature strengths in pursuit of goals: Effects on goal progress, need satisfaction, well-being, and implications for coaching psychologists. *International Coaching Psychology Review, 5,* 6 - 15.

Loewenstein, G., Schkade, D. (1999). *Well-being: The foundations of hedonic Psychology,* 85 – 105.

Lykken, D. & Tellengen, A. (1996). Happiness is a stochastic phenomenon. *Psychological Science, 7,* 186-89.

Lyubomirsky, S. (2007). *The how of happiness*. New York: Penguin.

Lyubomirsky, S. (2009). *Journal of Clinical Psychology, 65(5),* 467-489.

Maslow, A. (1954). *Motivation and Personality*. New York: Harper.

Maslow, A. (1968). *Toward a Psychology of being (2ⁿᵈed.)*. D. Van Nostrand.

Maslow, A. (1970). *Motivation and personality (2ⁿᵈ ed.)*. New York: Harper & Row.

Maslow, A. (1971). *A theory of Meta-motivation. The biological rooting of the value life*. In Farther reaches of human nature, 299-339, New York, NY: Viking, (Original work published in 1967).

Maslow, A. (1973). *Toward a psychology of being*. Englewood Cliffs, N.J.: Prentice-Hall.

Mastein, A.S. (2001). Ordinary magic: Resilience processes in development. *American Psychologist, 56,* 227-238.

Matthews, G., Deary, I. & Whiteman, M. (2009). *Personality traits*. (Third Edition). Cambridge: Cambridge University Press.

Mc Andrew, F.T., & Perilloux, C. (2012). The Selfish hero: A study of the individual benefits of self-sacrificial prosocial behaviour. *Psychological Reports, (1),* 27-43.

Meichenbaum, D. H., & Turk, D. (1982). Stress, coping and disease: A cognitive – behavioural perspective. In R.W.J. Newfield (Ed.). *Psychological stress and psychopathology,* 289-306. New York: Mc Graw – Hill.

Mongrain, M., & Anselmo-Matthews, T. (2012). Do positive psychology exercises work? A replication of Seligman et al. (2005). *Journal of Clinical Psychology, 4,* 382-389.

Myers, I.B. (1962). The Myers-Briggs type indicator. Princeton, NJ: Educational Testing Service.

Ness, L.S., & Segerstrom, S.C. (2006). Dispositional Optimism and coping: A meta-analytic review. *Personality and Social Psychology Review, 10.*

Park, N., & Peterson, C. (2006). Character strengths and happiness among young children: Content analysis of parental descriptions. *Journal of Happiness Study, 7,* 323-341.

Patnaik, G. (1988). *Psychology in Indian context.* In F.M. Sahoo (Ed.), Agra: National Psychological Corporation, 75 – 81.

Patnaik, G. (2017). *Personality and Positive Psychology.* Mental Health and Psychological well-being of adolescents, 235-249.

Peterson, C. (2006). A primer in positive psychology. New York: Oxford University Press.

Peterson, D.A., Kozhokar, D. (2017). *Peak-end effects for subjective mental workload ratings. Proc.* Hum. *61(1),* 2052-2056.

Peterson, C., & Seligman, M.E.P. (1987). Explanatory Style and Illness. *Journal of Personality, 55,* Issue 2.

Peterson, C., & Seligman, M.E.P. (2004). *Character strengths and virtues: A Handbook and Classification.* New York, NY: Oxford University Press.

Pietrowsky, R., & Mikutta, J. (2012). Effects of Positive Psychology interventions in depressive patients - A randomized control study. *Psychology, 3 (12),* 1067-1073.

Piliavin, J.A. (2003). Doing well by Doing Good: Benefits for the Benefactor. In C.L.M. Keyes and J. Haidt (Eds.), *Flourishing: Positive Psychology and the life well-lived.* Washington. DC: American Psychological Association.

Post, S.G. (2007). *Altruism and health. Perspectives from empirical research.* New York, NY: Oxford University Press.

Poulin, M.J., Brown, S.L., Dillard, A.J., & Smith, D.M. (2013). Giving to others and the association between stress and morality. *American Journal of Public Health, 103 (9)*, 1649-1655.

Privette, G. (1981). Dynamics of Peak performance. *Journal of Humanistic Psychology, 21(1)*, 57-67.

Quick, E.K. (2013). *Solution focused anxiety management. A treatment and training manual.* San Diego, CA: Elsevier Academic Press.

Robbins, B.D. (2008). What is the good life? Positive Psychology and renaissance of humanistic psychology. *The Humanistic Psychologist, 36*, 96-112.

Rogers, C.R. (1963). *The concept of the fully functioning person.* 17-26.

Rotter, J. (1966). Generalized expectancies for internal versus external control of reinforcement. *Psychological Monographs, 90*, 1-28.

Ryan, R.M., and E.L. Deci (2001). On happiness and human potentials: A Review of research on hedonic and eudaimonic well-being. *Annual Review of Psychology, 52*: 141-16.

Ryff, C.D., & Singer, B. (1998). *Psychological Inquiry, 9 (1)*, 1 – 28.

Ryff, C.D., & Singer, B. (2003). Flourishing under five: Resilience as a prototype of challenged thriving. In C.L.M. Keyes and J. Haidt (Eds.), *Flourishing: Positive Psychology and the life well-lived*, 15-36. American Psychological Association.

Salovey, P., & Mayer, J. (1990). Emotional intelligence. *Imagination, Cognition and personality, 9*, 185-211.

Schaffer, O. (2013). *Crafting Fun User Experiences: A method to Facilitate Flow,* Human Factors International.

Scheier, M.F., & Carver, C.S. (1985). Optimism, Coping and Health: Assessment and Implications of Generalized outcome Expectancies. *Health Psychology, 4(3),* 219-247.

Scheier, M.F., Weintraub, J.K., & Carver, C.S.(1986). Coping with stress: Divergent strategies of optimists and pessimists. *Journal of Personality and Social Psychology, 51,* 1257-1264.

Seear, K.H., Vella-Brodrick, D. (2013). Efficacy of positive psychology interventions to increase well-being: Examining the role of dispositional mindfulness. *Social Indicators Research, 114(3),* 1125-1141.

Seligman, M. (1984). *Journal of Personality and Social Psychology, 45(5),* 1136-1147.

Seligman, M. (2002). *Authentic happiness: Using the new positive psychology to realize your potential for lasting fulfilment.* Free Press.

Seligman, M. (2003). Positive Psychology: Fundamental assumptions. *The Psychologist,16(3),* 126-127.

Seligman, M. (2005). How to change your mind and your life. *American Psychologist,60(5),* 410.

Seligman, M. (2011). Flourish: *A visionary new understanding of happiness and well-being.* Free Press.

Seligman, M. (2012). *Flourish: A visionary new understanding of happiness and well-being.* New York, NY: Free Press.

Seligman, M., Steen, & Peterson, C. (2004). *Character strengths and virtues: A handbook and classifications, 1,* Oxford University Press.

Seligman, M., Steen, T.A., Park, N., & Peterson, C. (2005). Positive Psychology Progress: Empirical validation of interventions. *American Psychologist,60(5),* 410-421.

Sheldon, K.M., & King, L. (2001). Why positive psychology is necessary. *American Psychologist, 56 (3)*, 216 – 217.

Sheldon, K.M., & Lyubomirsky, S. (2006). How to increase and sustain positive emotion: The effects of expressing gratitude and visualizing best possible selves. *The Journal of Positive Psychology, 1(2)*, 73-82.

Snyder, C. R. (1994). *Handbook of hope.* Orlando, FL: Academic Press.

Snyder, C. R. (2000). *Handbook of hope.* Orlando, FL: Academic Press.

Stranger, M. (1999). *International review for the Sociology of Sport, 34 (3)*, 265 – 276.

Taylor, S.E. (1989). *Positive illusions: Creative self-deceptions and the healthy mind.* New York: Basic Books.

Taylor, S.E. & Gollwitzer, P.M. (1995). Effects of Mind-set on Positive Mind-set on positive Illusions. *Journal of Personality and Social Psychology, 59(2)*, 213-226.

Tiger, L. (1979). *Optimism: The Biology of Hope.* Simon & Schuster, New York.

Ullen, F., de Manzna, O., Almeida, R. et al., (2012). Proneness for psychological flow in everyday life: Associations with personality and intelligence. *Personality and Individual Differences, 52(2)*, 167-172.

Vaillant, G. (2000). Adaptive mental mechanisms: Their role in Positive Psychology. *American Psychologist, 55*, 89-98.

Velleman, J.D., (1991). Well-being and Time. Pacific Philosophical Quarterly, *72(1)*: 48-77.

Wallas, G. (1926). *The Art of thought.* London: Jonathan Cape.

Watkins, P.C. (2013*). Gratitude and the good life: Toward a psychology of appreciation.* New York, NY: Springer.

Watson, D., & Clark, L.A. (1984). Negative affectivity: The disposition to experience aversive emotional states. *Psychological Bulletin, 96,* 465-490.

Watson, D., & Pennebaker, J.W. (1989). Health complaints, stress, and distress: Exploring the central role of negative affectivity. *Psychological Review, 96,* 234-264.

Wills, TA. (1985). Stress, Social support, and the Buffering Hypothesis, *Psychological Bulletin, 98(2):* 310-57.

Wolpe, J. (1958). *Psychotherapy by reciprocal inhibition,* Stanford, CA: Stanford University Press.

Wood, A.M., Joseph, S., & Maltby, J. (2008). Gratitude uniquely predicts satisfaction with life: Incremental validity above the domains and facets of the five factor model. *Personality and Individual Difference, 45(1),* 49-59.

Zautra, A.J. (2003). *Emotions, stress, and health.* Oxford University Press.

Zunker, V.G. (2011). *Career Counselling: A holistic approach* (8[th]ed.). Belmont, CA: Brooks /Cole.